JERUSALEM: THE TRUTH

A compilation of editorials by
David Bar-Illan, Executive Editor
of *The Jerusalem Post*

ISBN: 1-930749-07-4

Printed in the United States of America

Table of Contents

The articles listed below were originally published in *The Jerusalem Post*, with the exception of "Assassination as National Trauma," which appeared in *The London Daily Telegraph*, and the final three articles, which were published in *The Levitt Letter*.

Introduction 2

Ominous Pronouncements 3
Olmert's First Test 4
Orient House 6
The Orient House Scandal 9
The Latest Jerusalem Probe 11
Credibility on Jerusalem 14
Don't Clog the Arteries 16
Abandoning "Greater Jerusalem" 18
Build Har Homa 21
Capital City 23
The Last Red Line 25
The Government's Euphemisms 28
Appeasement on Jerusalem 30
Olmert's Moment 32
Fire and Paralysis 34
The Continuing Battle 35
Security and Education 38
More Orient House Scandals 41
Secret Agreements on Jerusalem 43
Yielding on the Temple Mount 45
Contest of Wills Over Jerusalem 47
Toughness, Sensible and Otherwise 50
Talks and Bombs Combination 53

Close PA's Jerusalem Offices 56
Capitulation in Jerusalem 57
Jerusalem, Still to be Won 60
Indyk's Absence 63
Verbal Violence 65
U.S. Recognition of Jerusalem 68
Observers in Jerusalem 70
Jerusalem: Good and Bad News 73
A Black Day for the Whole Jewish Nation 75
World Statesman 76
Assassination as National Trauma 78
Wanted: A Healing 83
Negotiations Over Jerusalem 85
Security in Jerusalem 88
Shahal and Internal Security 89
The Election Festival 92
Frauds and Advocates 94
The Election Myth 96
The Jerusalem Negotiations 98
Jerusalem Divided 101
Incitement It is Not 104
The Orient House Dilemma 106
A Different Vision 108
The Terror Returns 111
Disappointing Speech 114
Needed: An Unconventional Response 116
The Awakening 120
Bravi, Weizman, Olmert 122
Charges Over Jerusalem 124
An *Evening Standard* Abomination 126
Appendix A: The Israeli-Palestinian Declaration of
Principles (Main Points) 133
Appendix B: Oslo Declaration 139

Appendix C: The PLO Charter 143
Preface to the Updated Edition 152
Archaeology Used to Bash Israel 152
Jerusalem at Disney World 156
Fighting the Last War 159
CNN: It's News to Me 162
The Press and Mrs. Clinton 166
Greatest Story Never Told 172
Invitation to Pressure 177
A Prelude to War 180
It's the Height of Hubris 183
Total Mobilization 186
The Battle for Jerusalem 191
Out of Sight, Out of Mind 196
David Bar-Illan Hospitalized After Heart Attack .. 200
Jerusalem: The Burdensome Stone 201
Jerusalem: The Cup of Trembling 205
American Airlines Flying Higher 207
From the Editor 209
About the Author 210

Introduction

What Israel intends to do about Jerusalem beggars belief and defies the laws of history.

For 2,000 years the Jewish people have prayed, every day of their existence, to return to Jerusalem. There is no precedent for such a bond between a people and a city in all the annals of mankind.

Since its founding by King David 3,000 years ago, Jerusalem has never been a capital of any other people. Mentioned close to 700 times in the Bible, and known also as Zion, it is the heart of Zionism. Without Jerusalem there can be no Israel, there can be no fulfillment of the Zionist dream of ingathering.

And yet, the government of Israel is now prepared to do what the governments of the world want it to do: relinquish half of Jerusalem — including the Old City and most of the holy places — to a PLO/Hamas state now taking shape at its side.

This is not what the government *says* it will do. On the contrary. It adamantly insists that Jerusalem will remain undivided under Israeli sovereignty as the eternal capital of Israel. But its deeds contradict its words. For the sake of what it believes will be a lasting peace, and driven by a vision of a New Middle East, Israel is on the way to cede half the city to a dictatorship. It is the first time in history that a free democracy voluntarily invites the establishment of a police state in the very heart of its most precious city on the hill.

In *The Jerusalem Post* editorials I tried to describe and explain how and why this is happening. I know that only by a world-wide awakening to the impending fateful blunder can Jerusalem hope to remain a free, democratic beacon of Judeo-Christian values. And I can only hope that the awareness and prayers of good people everywhere will help the world see the light.

Ominous Pronouncements

September 7, 1993

One of the scourges of Israeli politics is the tendency of government officials to speak out of turn. For example, as education minister, Shulamit Aloni proved especially prone to saying the wrong thing at the wrong time; this past spring her remarks nearly caused a coalition crisis.

But the public has learned that many such pronouncements, especially on current policies, are neither wishful thinking nor the personal ruminations of frustrated politicians. Often they are inadvertent disclosures of secret decisions made by officials who cannot contain themselves. A declaration by Police Minister Moshe Shahal, for example, about Israel's willingness to relinquish the whole Golan cannot be taken lightly. Knowing of Shahal's closeness to Prime Minister Yitzhak Rabin, one suspects it reflects more than one minister's personal opinion.

Similarly, it would be foolhardy to dismiss pronouncements made on Sunday by Deputy Foreign Minister Yossi Beilin and other Labor party officials. Lecturing before "Mashov," the circle of dovish Labor party members, Beilin recommended a partition of Jerusalem into quarters, one of which would be administered by the Palestinians. The inexorable implication is that this "quarter" would become what the PLO is demanding: the capital of the Palestinian state.

Beilin's words drew an immediate condemnation from Mayor Teddy Kollek, who said a divided administration in Jerusalem is unthinkable. But Kollek's protest would be more credible had Kollek himself not been the one who conceived the "quarters" idea some time ago. Beilin's suggestion becomes even more ominous against the background of reports that Rabin has told associates that Kollek's re-election is essential to "making a deal with the Palestinians on Jerusalem."

Just as portentous were declarations by various high officials that the agreement with the PLO would inevitably lead to a Palestinian state. MK [Member of the Knesset] Avraham Burg, a leading Labor dove, on Sunday demanded that like-minded party members openly declare support for a Palestinian state. Labor party doves are now bragging that while they were considered extremist not long ago, the policies they were espousing have now become mainstream. "Now is the time we again occupy our place on the left of the mainstream, and lead the way to a Palestinian state," Burg said.

Ambassador Itamar Rabinovich also declared on Sunday that the agreement will probably lead to a Palestinian state within five years. And, needless to say, Faisal Husseini keeps assuring his audiences that the imminent Israeli evacuation of Gaza and Jericho is but a first step towards a Palestinian state.

Many in Israel, probably a large majority, would consider "getting rid" of Gaza a blessing, though they may not have thought out all the implications of the move. The number of those who care just as little about Jericho is probably not much smaller. But the majority may not be enthusiastic about the agreement if they knew that the Gaza/Jericho package is but a euphemism for a Palestinian state with part of Jerusalem as its capital.

Olmert's First Test

January 5, 1994

The current arguments about the size of the projected self-rule area in Jericho may have caused a mini-crisis in the Israel-PLO negotiations. But both sides know the decisive showdown will be not over Jericho, Gaza or any of the administered territories, but Jerusalem. No Arab leader today will agree to what Israel considers a sine qua non: full Israeli sovereignty over an undivided Jerusalem. Hence it matters little what concessions the government is willing to make in other areas. If it insists, as it is sworn to do, on sovereignty over all of Jerusalem, it will not satisfy Arab demands nor have a "final status" agreement with the PLO.

That is why those who favor a division of the city protest against every project which increases Jewish presence in the part of Jerusalem occupied by Jordan between 1948 and 1967. The foreign press often refers to this section of the city as "Arab Jerusalem," though it already has a Jewish majority; and members of the "peace camp," many of whom consider the division of the city unavoidable, fiercely oppose changes in the city's demographics. They claim, as they did yesterday, that since Israel has agreed to negotiate the matter of Jerusalem when the final status is discussed, such changes would "put spokes in the wheel of peace."

This argument has reached absurd proportions with the protest against a small construction project on the Mount of Olives. A small tract of land (seven dunams [roughly 2 acres]), on which the Beit Orot Yeshiva [Hebrew school] is now located, was purchased by a Jewish landowner in 1985. But in 1988, during the previous city administration, the city planning department recommended that the land be expropriated for an Arab school, which would serve the village of A-Sawana. Yet for the following five years nothing was done about building the school.

The new city administration under Ehud Olmert, reversing the previous administration, decided on Monday that the yeshiva had a right to build on this land, which is, after all, its backyard. Representatives of Meretz [an Israeli government party] and the One Jerusalem party fiercely objected, but the administration easily carried the day.

Neither side made a secret of its agenda. Deputy Mayor

Shmuel Meir (NRP) said approval of the project reflected the new city administration's plans to increase the Jewish presence in that part of the city. The opposition plainly wanted to prevent precisely such an increase.

Both sides realize that the Arab school issue is a red herring. The school can easily be built nearby, on the many vacant tracts in the area. But it seems to be in the nature of things in Jerusalem that such minor issues become part of the national debate.

There should be no doubt that the yeshiva has a right to build on the land. That Jews should be prevented to build homes anywhere they want in Jerusalem is utterly unthinkable. But it is also unconscionable to let political considerations hold up the construction of an Arab school for A-Sawana. Olmert has vowed to keep Jerusalem undivided, and he has overwhelming public support for this. But he should also fulfill his promise to provide the Arab residents of this city with all the facilities and amenities they are due.

Orient House
February 23, 1994

Not too long ago, there was almost total agreement in Israel on the very minimum the country must retain to make any peace settlement acceptable. Often cited by these minimalists was David Ben-Gurion, who in his last years favored relinquishing most of the land won in the 1967 war. He said Israel must keep all of Jerusalem and the Golan Heights.

Until the last Knesset elections, the Labor Party deemed this minimalist formula less than satisfactory. It took for granted retaining the Golan and Jerusalem, and wanted to keep more than a quarter of Judea and Samaria, as stipulated in the

Alon Plan. No one in the party - least of all Prime Minister Yitzhak Rabin - ever expressed readiness to leave the Golan and split Jerusalem.

This is no longer true. An apparent majority in the party views the Golan as dispensable, and even on Jerusalem the consensus seems to be cracking. Deputy Foreign Minister Yossi Beilin, the father of the Oslo agreement, has proposed Palestinian control of part of the city. Many in his party concur.

But the danger to Jerusalem's unity under Israeli sovereignty lurks not so much in Beilin's words as in Arab deeds. The Palestinian Arabs have learned from Zionist history that the most effective way to achieve political goals is to establish facts on ground, preferably in low-profile increments. One application of this lesson is unfolding in the Jordan Valley. Imitating the Zionist pioneers who believed that every cultivated acre and every new settlement helped reinforce the national claim to the land, Arab squatters are now illegally settling near the Israeli villages. Their intention is clear: to establish an irreversible Arab majority in an area even some of Israel's doves consider vital for its security.

In Jerusalem, where the ultimate fate of the Declaration of Principles may be determined, Arab tactics are more sophisticated. In 1980, the Palestinians registered Orient House, a large building compound in the American Colony section of the city, as a home for the "Institute for Arab Research," a foundation headed by Faisal Husseini. Over the years they have transformed it into a combination military headquarters, government seat, and foreign affairs ministry of the PLO.

Both the government and the municipality have chosen to ignore the nature of Orient House activities. But the PLO, which uses the compound as its local headquarters, has raised it to international status by receiving official guests there, including the American secretary of state and the French foreign minister, and by signing international agreements, including the agreement for a U.S. grant for the autonomous areas. The PLO has thus made it function as the political and diplomatic "capital" of the territories.

It has also given Orient House the aura of an armed-forces headquarters, by decorating it with military paraphernalia and posting its own security men around the building. When the newly recruited Palestine Police officers arrived in town, the PLO used the place for a military reception for them.

On Monday, Likud MKs protested against the apparent extraterritorial status of the building. It seems to be off-limits to demonstrations: the police assiduously keep protesters - both Arab and Jewish - away from the building. The officials inside oversee activities intended to assert Arab sovereignty in the eastern part of the city: marches of masked men, and night-time road blocks in its neighborhood, where PLO security personnel act as if they were a police force. Most tellingly, the building seems exempt from city real estate taxes, a privilege reserved for embassies and consulates. It has not paid a bill of over NIS 500,000 it owes the municipality.

When confronted with these facts on Monday, Police Minister Moshe Shahal denied that the building and its residents have special privileges. "If the police suspect something illegal is going on there," he said, "I will not prevent them from going in." Alerted to the goings on, last week Prime Minister Rabin warned that if the PLO declared Orient House its foreign ministry, he would consider the Oslo agreement void.

But the fact is that there is no way of ensuring there are no illegal activities in Orient House unless the police enter the building. Nor does it make sense to threaten that if the PLO calls the building by an official name, dire consequences will follow. The PLO has already established this Jerusalem building as a seat of government, and unless Israel reverses the process, and the Jerusalem Municipality begins to treat it truly as "just another building" by collecting all taxes due, Orient House will be recognized as the Palestinian White House by the world community.

At that point the solemn pledge "to keep Jerusalem as the unified capital of Israel forever," so readily made by all government leaders from Ben-Gurion on down, will seem like a fond, wistful memory.

The Orient House Scandal
July 7, 1994

At first glance, Prime Minister Yitzhak Rabin's indignation at the opposition's charge that he is wavering on the indivisibility of Jerusalem seems justified. Both he and Foreign Minister Shimon Peres have repeatedly, clearly, and forcefully said that Jerusalem is the eternal capital of Israel, and that it will stay undivided under Israeli sovereignty. Moreover, the Oslo Declaration of Principles stipulates that the fate of the city will not be negotiated during the two years of the interim period.

Indeed, Rabin and Peres can hardly be blamed for demanding to know what more they can say to reassure Israelis they have no intention of satisfying Yasser Arafat's wishes by relinquishing part of Jerusalem to the Palestinian entity. But nor can the public be blamed for treating these solemn pledges with skepticism.

One reason for doubt is that Rabin has made similar pledges in the past, only to ignore them as soon as they threatened to impede progress in the "peace process." Rabin has said that Israel would withdraw from the agreement with Arafat if the PLO failed to abrogate its covenant; or if Arafat's own Fatah [his branch of the PLO] perpetrated terrorist acts; or if

Arafat called himself "president of Palestine;" or if Orient House in Jerusalem acted as the Palestinian Authority's foreign ministry. He has denied the existence of secret agreements with the PLO and a secret letter about Jerusalem, vowed no terrorists convicted of killing Israelis would be released, denied that known murderers would be allowed to join the Palestinian police, and that Arafat has been promised a Jerusalem visit. All these pledges, promises, and denials have proved false.

Another disquieting factor is the Palestinian talent for unobtrusively establishing "facts on the ground." The techniques recall those used by the pre-state Yishuv [Jewish settlement], and seem just as effective. Orient House in Jerusalem is a typical example. Begun as an information center and an unofficial headquarters of the Palestinian half of the Jordanian-Palestinian delegation to the Madrid peace talks, it has gradually turned into the foreign ministry of the Palestinian entity - precisely the kind of transformation Rabin warned would cause Israel's withdrawal from the agreement.

This development is puzzling, not only because it mocks Rabin's warning, but because it belies what Faisal Husseini told *The Jerusalem Post* only last week. When asked about his plans for Orient House, he insisted that the offices there would restrict themselves to services to the Arab community in Jerusalem, and that all political and diplomatic activities on behalf of the Palestinian Authority would emanate from Gaza or Jericho.

Yet on Tuesday, MK Eliahu Ben-Elissar (Likud) brought to light a letter dated June 30 and signed by Husseini on Orient House stationery, which was distributed to all diplomatic representatives in this country by Ivory Coast Ambassador Jean-Pierre Boni, dean of the diplomatic corps in Israel. In it Husseini gives specific guidelines to "all countries present in this area" wishing to greet "President Arafat" on his arrival in

Gaza. These include a request to have the interested governments send directly to Orient House, by fax, the names of the diplomatic representatives wishing to meet Arafat, and details of their vehicles, drivers, and accompanying entourage.

That the dean of the diplomatic corps should treat Husseini's request as if it had come from a foreign minister of a sovereign state may be improper, but it is hardly surprising. The Israeli government, to which Boni is accredited, seems to do no less. For all its warnings that centers of activity in Jerusalem on behalf of the Authority will be shut down, and despite Rabin's threat to "call the whole agreement off" if Orient House acted as a foreign ministry, the fact is that the Israeli government is tolerating, if not encouraging, such activity in Jerusalem.

It is only natural, then, that despite Rabin's protestations the public views these developments as steps toward turning eastern Jerusalem into the capital of a Palestinian state.

The Latest Jerusalem Probe
August 12, 1994

Faisal Husseini, who is the Palestinian Authority's "minister for Jerusalem," is testing the government's resolve. By inviting representatives of foreign countries to his headquarters in Jerusalem's Orient House to discuss the freeing of funds for the Palestinian Authority, he clearly violated the Declaration of Principles and the Gaza/Jericho First agreement. The agreements clearly state that the authority's institutions must be confined to the self-rule areas.

As the government has repeatedly declared, Orient House can function as an institution serving local cultural, educational, and welfare needs. It cannot act as an agency of the authority, and it certainly must not function as a foreign ministry. In fact, Prime Minister Yitzhak Rabin has said that if it did, "the whole Israel-PLO agreement will be rendered null and void."

Understandably, Foreign Minister Shimon Peres would like to minimize the importance of Husseini's official meetings with foreign diplomats. Perfunctorily, he has asked his ministry's legal adviser to determine whether these meetings were legal, but added that they were anyway marginal and unnecessary. Impatient to get on with "the process," he obviously views such violations as little more than awkward nuisances. Like the inauspicious calls by Yasser Arafat for Jihad and by his "foreign minister" Farouk Kaddoumi for the destruction of Israel, they must not get in the way of progress.

But it would be foolish for the government to underestimate the cumulative effect of relatively "minor" violations of the agreement. That under Israeli and American pressure, a needy and desperate Arafat consents to say that Kaddoumi's pronouncements are "incompatible with the spirit of the agreement" is hardly an indication of the revulsion and condemnation one had a right to expect of the PLO chief. That Kaddoumi is still the PLO's "foreign minister" and No. 2 in the organization speaks louder than the refined diplomatic language with which Arafat has chosen to chastise him.

Similarly, the impression of the latest Orient House incident is that representatives of foreign nations come to the Palestinian center in Jerusalem without hesitation when summoned by Husseini; that they raise the PLO flag on their cars when they travel in the eastern part of the city; that in Jerusalem, Israel's declared capital, they are guarded by the unofficial but highly visible Palestinian secret service; that they appear at Husseini's office to discuss matters of state without coordination with, let alone permission from the Israeli government; and that they report about their meetings not to their embassies in Tel Aviv, but directly to the foreign ministries in their capitals. If there is any difference between the way they treat Orient House from the way they treat Israel's Foreign Ministry, it is not readily apparent to the naked eye.

To ignore the Palestinian efforts to establish political facts in Jerusalem is to play ostrich. With assiduity and persistence, the PLO is developing a bureaucratic, political infrastructure intended to present the world with a de facto Palestinian capital in the city by the time the "final status" talks begin in 1996. As PLO spokeswoman at the UN Fadah Abdel Haddi put it in June, "It is unrealistic for Israel to believe that it can hold on to all of Jerusalem. Jerusalem is a Palestinian center, not only religiously but politically. Much of the activity of the Palestinian Authority is planned and executed in Jerusalem."

Nor is Husseini's "foreign ministry" at Orient House the only Palestinian quasi-governmental office in town. Only yesterday Peace Watch, a non-partisan organization dedicated to monitoring the implementation of the Israel-PLO agreement, discovered another institution in Jerusalem directly connected with the Palestinian Authority.

It is called The Palestinian Energy Center, and billed as a "national institution under the supervision of the National Palestinian Authority." According to its charter, its "initial start-up costs, the operation costs, and the direct costs are covered by the budget allocated to the center by the European Commission, the Palestinian National Authority, and by the funds raised from international cooperation."

There are at least three other major Palestinian institutions in Jerusalem closely connected with the Palestinian Authority: the Palestinian Economic Council for Development and Recovery (PECDAR), the Palestinian Radio and Television Authority, and the Palestinian Center for Statistics. All are supported by the international community.

That these institutions are internationally funded is hardly surprising. Most governments favor the evolvement of eastern Jerusalem into a capital of the Palestinian state. And if the government is serious about keeping all of Jerusalem under Israeli sovereignty, it will have to treat efforts to convert it into a Palestinian capital less flippantly.

Husseini's move is just the latest PLO probe in the campaign against Israel's intention to keep Jerusalem its undivided capital. It is not a campaign in which the PLO is alone. Its idea of "two capitals in one city" - a prescription for the redivision of the city - has international as well as Israeli support. It cannot be countered by the wave of a minister's hand. Only firm insistence on Palestinian adherence to the spirit and the letter of the Oslo and Cairo agreements can prevent an irreversible deterioration in Israel's position in Jerusalem.

Credibility on Jerusalem
November 6, 1994

Prime Minister Yitzhak Rabin's unequivocal declaration on Jerusalem at the Casablanca conference must have buoyed the vast majority of Israelis. According to all polls and voting patterns, keeping Jerusalem undivided and under Israeli sovereignty is an article of faith for over 80 percent of the population. That Rabin reiterated the government's commitment to this principle in the presence of President Bill Clinton at the Knesset, and then again in a Casablanca forum filled with Arab delegations, gave his words unprecedented credibility.

The only trouble with such statements is that they are belied by what is happening in Jerusalem itself. The Palestinians have learned that facts speak louder than words. And the facts they are establishing in Jerusalem are slowly eroding Israeli authority in the eastern part of the city.

Recent events make this erosion all too clear. When the

PLO said that Clinton would not be welcome at the Temple Mount if he arrived accompanied by Mayor Ehud Olmert, the visit was canceled. The cancellation of the visit, a clear surrender to Palestinian threats, was an unprecedented American move: both presidents Richard Nixon and Jimmy Carter assumed on their visits to Jerusalem that being accompanied by the elected mayor of the city was unexceptionable.

Yesterday, Turkey's Prime Minister Tancu Ciller visited the Temple Mount without the mayor. The official reason was that Olmert does not accompany guests on Shabbat [the Sabbath], but the absence of any Israeli official in Ciller's party makes the deference to Palestinian wishes transparent. Worse, when Ciller arrived at Orient House, a building the PLO and most of the world consider the Palestinian's government house, Israeli security men accompanying her were forcefully prevented from entering. It was impossible not to recall Rabin's threat that if the PLO used Orient House as a foreign ministry, the whole peace process would come to a halt.

Nor are these isolated incidents. The week ended with a clear PLO victory over the Jordanians in the matter of the Moslem holy places. It can be argued that whether the Hashemite Kingdom or the PLO controls the holy Moslem sites should be of little concern to Israel. But the fact is that the PLO managed to overturn by force a solemn Israeli commitment to Jordan.

In the Israel-Jordan peace treaty, Israel is pledged to preserve the Hashemite privileged status on the Temple Mount. But when Jordan recently appointed Abdel Kader Abdeen as "Mufti" (the ultimate religious authority in Jerusalem) the PLO countered with the appointment of Akhrima Sabri - a Wakf [Moslem religious council] official formerly on Jordan's payroll and now an Arafat man - as its own mufti.

The PLO security services, whose authority is presumably limited to Gaza and Jericho, then threatened with physical harm anyone who would knock on Abdeen's door. Not surprisingly, no one dared defy PLO security chief Jibril Rajoub, whom Israel has allowed to extend his authority to the whole "West Bank." And Abdeen - finding himself unemployed - soon stopped showing up in his office. Moreover, the Hebrew daily *Ha'aretz* reported on Friday that Rajoub has also warned that if King Hussein visits Jerusalem, his fate would be similar to that of his assassinated grandfather, King Abdallah.

The Hashemites, being realists and survivors if nothing else, were quick to recognize the "facts on the ground." Realizing that Israel was not about to live up to its commitment, both Prince Hassan and Jordan's Prime Minister Abdel Salim Majali promised that they would hand over religious rights in Jerusalem to the PLO as soon as the final status talks establish Palestinian authority in the city.

That Israel could so easily allow its pledge to Jordan to be overturned by Rajoub's henchmen hardly enhances Israeli credibility. And the inability of Israeli officials and security personnel to enter either religious or secular areas in Jerusalem mocks pronouncements on eternal Israeli sovereignty in the city. Indeed, such retreat in the face of Palestinian pressure even before negotiations on the city have begun seems to indicate that Rabin's vows on Jerusalem should not be taken any more seriously than his oath never to relinquish the Golan.

Don't Clog the Arteries
November 29, 1994

More than any other Israeli city, Jerusalem presents a daily challenge to the concept of coexistence. That its population is three-quarters Jewish and one-quarter Arab, and that both peoples claim the city as their capital, may be Jerusalem's most acute problem, but it is by no means the only one.

The number of different religions and denominations is staggering, and the intensity of the antagonisms between them is often astonishing. That life in Jerusalem is nevertheless as calm as it is, and that the level of violence and the number of homicides are dramatically lower than in most cities in the world is one of Israel's most outstanding miracles.

What has made this miracle possible is a policy, initiated by Teddy Kollek, of maintaining a delicate balance between Jerusalem's different communities. True, even Kollek's inimitable diplomatic talents could not completely overcome the passions of the intifada [the Palestinian uprising against Israeli rule]. But he did manage to keep violence to a minimum, and he prevented friction between secular and haredi [religiously observant] Jews from making life in the city intolerable.

It is a tribute to Kollek's skills that his successor, Ehud Olmert, has attempted to continue his intercommunal policies. But now the delicate balance is being threatened by the haredi demand to close Bar-Ilan Street on Shabbat. For Olmert, who owes his election to haredi support, it will not be easy to resist such a demand. But if he wishes the city to remain livable for secular Jews, he had better reject it out of hand.

There is nothing wrong, of course, with closing streets in haredi neighborhoods on Shabbat. On the contrary - in areas where the vast majority of the residents are observant, religious sensibilities should be respected. It is only fitting that such neighborhoods be allowed to preserve their character. At most, such traffic restrictions may cause minor inconveniences to the non-observant and non-Jews.

But Bar-Ilan street is not a side street in a religious neighborhood. It is a main Jerusalem artery, around which a religious community has proliferated. Closing this artery for a period of more than 24 hours every week will cause not only major inconveniences, but real danger to a vast number of Jerusalem residents. The street is the main link to Ramat Eshkol, French Hill and other non-religious neighborhoods, and it services the Hadassah University Hospital on Mount Scopus. One can always find alternative, circuitous ways to travel, but those, too, may be subject to closure if religious residents, following the Bar-Ilan precedent, demand it.

What Olmert must make clear is that it is one thing to accommodate religious residents in their own neighborhoods by closing off their streets to Shabbat traffic, and quite another to shut off a main city artery. Any concession to the haredi community on this will destroy the delicate balance between the communities, accelerate the departure of "secular" Jews from the city, and destroy Jerusalem's unique character as the pluralistic and tolerant capital of Israel.

Abandoning "Greater Jerusalem"
January 20, 1995

There is something disingenuous about the government's strenuous efforts to deny the existence of "Greater Jerusalem" as a geographic entity and security concept. It is, after all, the Labor Party which gave the term its currency. Advocates of Jewish presence throughout Judea, Samaria and Gaza have never differentiate between the Jerusalem environs and those of Hebron or Gaza.

Labor's insistence on making the "Jerusalem region" separate and different was reflected in the party's platform of 1992. It asserted that "Israel will keep vital territory not heavily populated by Arabs, such as the Jerusalem environs and the Etzion bloc ... New settlements will not be established and existing ones will not be expanded, except in the Jerusalem area and the Jordan Valley." Indeed, distinguishing between "security settlements" - those near Jerusalem, in the Jordan Valley and the Golan - and "political settlements" - those in other parts of the territories - became Yitzhak Rabin's election-campaign slogan and "red line" par excellence. Nor was the concept abandoned after the elections. It was reiterated in a government decision in January 1993, which mentioned "Greater Jerusalem" as a region of national priority, where development will be encouraged and supported.

At first glance, the reason Rabin has decided to depart from this concept is that he felt he had to yield to threats by his coalition partner, the Meretz party. (Strangely, the Meretz ministers - who often decry the way the minority haredi parties impose their will on the country - seem to have no compunction about forcing their own agenda on a weak government.) But the more fundamental reason for Rabin's readiness to ignore his most cherished security precepts is that he does not believe he can continue the peace process and bolster settlements at the same time. This is not because the Declaration of Principles dictates the freezing of settlements. It does not. It is because Rabin is convinced that Yasser Arafat, on whose collaboration progress in the talks depends, will lose credibility among Palestinians if settlement expansion continues.

The injustice of freezing the settlements is self-evident. No community can be "frozen." Families bring children into the world, they are joined by relatives from other areas of the country or from abroad, they become more affluent, and they need to expand. They must build not only homes but schools, synagogues, community centers and sport facilities. As one commentator put it, to freeze a community means to put it into a sealed room until the oxygen runs out.

Indeed, the notion that the Jewish communities in Judea,

Samaria and Gaza can be put into a state of suspended anima-
tion until the final status of the territories is determined is as
absurd as demanding that the Arab communities in the territories become inert until a final agreement is reached. There
is feverish building in Arab towns and villages, supported by
Hamas and the PLO, and totally uncontrolled by the government. No one objects, and no one protests.

Yet for all the unfairness in this imbalance, Rabin may be
justified in feeling that the Oslo process will die if Jewish
home construction - even if only in the townships around
Jerusalem - is allowed to continue. What must be recognized
is that not only the Palestinians and the Israeli Left expect the
DOP [Declaration of Principles] to lead to a Palestinian state
on the 1967 lines. The whole world does. And if the land on
which the Jewish towns and villages now stand is going to be
part of this state, the right of Jewish residents to build on their
property seems irrelevant. The world community fully expects them to abandon their homes and move away once the
final agreement is reached.

Rabin may still be nursing the hope that Israel will be
able to keep some of the towns around Jerusalem in a final
arrangement. But the message he has sent by stopping public
construction in these towns is unmistakable: these areas are
part of the Palestinian entity.

The very fact that he has promised to inform the Palestinian Authority of any exceptional construction the government
will make, the rescinding of Israeli authority over some of the
state lands, and the pledge not to appropriate state land except to build security roads - all these signal a tacit recognition of eventual Palestinian ownership. As Jerusalem Mayor
Ehud Olmert put it yesterday, it would be far more honest if
the government openly announced that it intends to retreat to
the 1967 lines.

Perhaps most disturbing is the realization that the very

same rationalization used for crossing the red line on the "Greater Jerusalem" issue will have to be used when metropolitan Jerusalem comes up in the negotiations on the final status.

The Palestinians are far more adamant about getting at least part of the city (as a first step) than they are about possessing Efrat and Ma'aleh Adumim. To bring the Oslo agreement to its logical and successful conclusion, half of Jerusalem will also have to be given up. And once the Palestinians realize that for the Rabin government the success of the process far outweighs even the most hallowed "red lines," they will consider no demands unthinkable.

Build Har Homa
February 3, 1995

The Jerusalem planning committee's decision to approve the immediate construction of 6,500 new housing units at Har Homa in southern Jerusalem is a welcome development. But it is bound to put the resolve of both city and government to a test.

The land on which these units will be built has been expropriated from Jews, but Arabs from the neighboring areas have threatened to stop construction. As adviser to Yasser Arafat, Salah Ta'amri, a resident of the area, put it on Wednesday, "This is our land . . . We shall stop the bulldozers with our bodies." The Jewish Gush Shalom group, which in past weeks joined Palestinian demonstrators against Jewish building in Judea and Samaria, has called the move "a gross provocation against peace." This, despite the city's intention to build 3,500 housing units for Palestinians in the same neighborhood. Clearly, what the Palestinians and Gush Shalom fear is that the Har Homa development will prevent the eastern part of the city from becoming the capital of a Palestinian state.

There are other, non-political objections to the plan. Private developer David Myr, who has devoted 25 years to planning a construction project in the area and attracting investors, vehemently opposes government intervention. With good reason, he wonders why the neighborhood cannot·be developed strictly by private entrepreneurs.

Newly installed city engineer Uri Ben-Asher has other objections. He bitterly complains that political, rather than urban development, considerations have motivated the decision. Expressing an opinion shared by many Jerusalemites, he says the city resembles "a man with clogged arteries, all fat on the outside and a weak heart in the middle."

His objections to the proposed Har Homa plans may be all too valid. But Jerusalem cannot be treated as just another city. In the battle to keep it undivided under Israeli rule, the building of Har Homa may be a decisive move. Whether the neighborhood becomes Jewish or mixed, it will make the division of the city virtually impossible. As committee chairman Uri Lupoliansky said on Wednesday, "These plans are important for strengthening Jerusalem as the capital of Israel and the Jewish people."

Since all appeals against the project have been rejected by the High Court, there is nothing to prevent work from beginning as soon as the city council and the district planning commission approve the plans. Now it must be hoped that neither bureaucratic impediments, nor political considerations, nor threats by Palestinian officials and their Israeli allies will hold back this enterprise.

Capital City
May 9, 1995

Israel's 47th Independence Day was less than a week ago but it appears the meaning of independence has escaped some government ministers - apparently even the prime minister himself. Some last-minute lobbying by an "unnamed official traveling with Prime Minister Yitzhak Rabin's entourage" against today's congressional initiative to move the U.S. Embassy to Jerusalem is not merely embarrassing, but reminiscent of the traditional behavior of Diaspora Jews [those who live outside of Israel] in times of trouble.

The "don't make waves" approach to life may have been suitable for a persecuted minority living in hostile surroundings. The establishment of the State of Israel, with Jerusalem as its capital, was intended to consign this philosophy of Jewish life to the dustbin of history. In the nearly half-century of its existence, Israel has indeed changed the image - and self-image - of the Jewish people, immeasurably and for the better.

Most countries with whom Israel has diplomatic relations may have chosen to dispute the fact that Jerusalem is legitimately the country's capital but this slight is not one Israelis should choose to ignore. This is not a pariah state, nor does it depend on the whims of others for its survival. As the only democracy in the Middle East, it deserves the respect that other countries, including some of the worst tyrannical dictatorships, take for granted. It is the right of any sovereign state to choose its own capital.

U.S. Ambassador to Israel Martin Indyk has said moving the U.S. Embassy to Jerusalem would explode the peace process and Secretary of State Warren Christopher added over the weekend that such a move would "interfere" with it. It is difficult to see how. If the Palestinians and Syrians are sincere about making peace with Israel - and there are still serious questions about their final intentions - the siting of the U.S. Embassy in the western part of Jerusalem should not raise an eyebrow in Gaza or Damascus.

Rabin correctly pointed out that world recognition of Israeli sovereignty over a united Jerusalem is the government's main goal. It is curious that he does not accept that moving the American Embassy to Jerusalem can only strengthen this aim. Once the powerful U.S. moves its embassy, other countries are sure to follow suit, leading to a strong diplomatic presence in Israel's capital that would bolster the city's status.

Even more puzzling is the suggestion that moving the U.S. Embassy is a Likud ploy to sabotage the peace process. For decades, Israeli officials and pro-Israeli lobbyists in Washington of all political stripes have been pushing for recognition of Jerusalem as the nation's capital. To suggest suddenly that a congressional initiative, which apparently has the support of 93 senators, is the work of partisan Israeli politicians or their American supporters smacks more of paranoia than reason.

Senate Majority Leader Robert Dole, the sponsor of the initiative, and Democratic Senator Daniel Inouye, who has announced he will cosponsor Dole's move, must find it bewildering that the leader of a proud, independent nation should be so suspicious of their efforts on Israel's behalf. They probably also fail to understand how important ministers like Avraham Shohat and Yossi Sarid can claim, as they did after Sunday's cabinet meeting, that the siting of the American embassy in Israel is "clearly an internal American matter" as Sarid put it or, as Shulamit Aloni remarked, "provocative." The words of the psalmist "If I forget thee, O Jerusalem," which resonated so strongly over the ages, ironically now seem forgotten at a time when Israel's economic, diplomatic and military standing is stronger than ever before.

The issue of Israel's capital is an Israeli issue, and only an Israeli issue. It is in Israel's interests, not America's, that the U.S. Embassy be situated in Jerusalem. One would expect the country's leaders to understand this and to strengthen, rather than disparage, the standing of their capital.

The Last Red Line
May 26, 1995

If this week's debate over the expropriation of land in Jerusalem has made one thing clear, it is that the government's capacity for discarding its own "red lines" is limitless.

To avowed pragmatists this may seem a wise course. After all, some of the Labor Party's most fundamental articles of faith - that Israel should never negotiate with the PLO, withdraw from the Golan, or allow the establishment of a Palestinian state - have been effectively broken without an earthshaking upheaval. If anything, the shattering of these taboos, whose advocates hope will bring peace, has made Labor's leaders the world's darlings. There is no reason, then, to suppose that another sacred tenet - that Jerusalem must stay the undivided capital of Israel - cannot be forfeited with impunity.

The clamor against "rigidity" on Jerusalem has already begun. In what has become a routine way to prepare the public for changes in government policy, articles by government-supporting commentators now explain why peace can only be achieved if Jerusalem is divided (the current euphemism is "shared"), so that it can serve both as the capital of Israel and the capital of the Palestinian state.

One of the rationalizations for a redivision of the city is that it is not truly united even now. There are areas in it where

Jews fear to tread (paradoxically, there are no sections which Arabs avoid), and where the ambience is unmistakably Arab. It will not be a great loss, say these observers, if the demarcation line becomes official.

All sorts of suggestions have been put forward. One plan, supported by Deputy Foreign Minister Yossi Beilin (often the harbinger of government policy changes), is to divide the city into boroughs which will be municipally connected but under different sovereignties. Others speak of a single capital "for two nations and three religions."

What the these suggestions have in common is detachment from reality. A city can work as two separate entities, as Jerusalem and Berlin did. But it cannot belong to two sovereignties and remain united. Jerusalem is not like an American town which can sit astride a state border, one half in Texas and one in Arkansas. A city with two totally different systems of government, different sets of laws and law enforcement apparatuses would find it difficult to function even if the two sovereignties were democratic. To suppose that it could be a unified city and serve both a democratic government and a police state is nothing short of ludicrous.

But the most worrisome argument used by advocates of the city's redivision is that the surgery is essential for the achievement of peace. There can be no peace with the

Palestinians and the Arab world, they say, unless at least part of Jerusalem becomes the capital of a Palestinian state. But once this assumption is allowed to dictate Israel's moves, the country becomes a hostage to extortion. If attaining Arab willingness to sign a peace treaty is the supreme goal, to which all else is subordinated, there can be no limit to Israeli concessions, and indeed no "red lines" and no taboos.

This week's political maneuvers were but a taste of things to come. The government reversed itself on a matter which it considered crucial. It cajoled the Clinton administration to cast the first American veto in five years at the UN Security Council to defeat a relatively mild resolution against the land appropriations. It then did a turnabout, not because it truly feared being toppled, but because it assumed - perhaps correctly - that the peace process would be endangered by the expropriations.

Clearly, the Arab parties' no-confidence motion was not what panicked the government. On the contrary, the government obviously welcomed the move as an pretext for climbing down the expropriation tree. What gave it pause was the threat of the resumption of the intifada (a euphemism for PLO terrorism), the prospect of a freeze in relations with Arab countries, and the possibility Syria would not resume talks.

Housing Minister Binyamin Ben-Eliezer has called the day the government surrendered on the expropriation a black day in the country's history. To assuage his own concerns and those of the majority of the nation he announced the building of thousands of housing units in the eastern part of Jerusalem in the near future. But the same considerations which begat the government's surrender this week will prevail when Arab threats to abort the peace process accompany the appearance of the first bulldozers anywhere in eastern Jerusalem. That the government will yield again is a foregone conclusion.

It seems clear now why the government has agreed with the PLO to postpone talks on the fate of Jerusalem to the last phase of the negotiations. As all polls indicate, a vast majority of Israelis consider the taboo on the division of Jerusalem the most sacred of all. If redividing the city is ever to prove palatable, the government seems to believe, the Israeli insistence on keeping the whole city under Israeli sovereignty must appear as the only remaining obstacle to peace.

But it requires extraordinary gullibility to believe that the PLO and the Arab regimes, acutely aware of their extortionate powers after this week's victory, will be satisfied with half of Jerusalem, and live peacefully with Israel ever after. An extortionist, whose appetite does not grow by what it feeds on, is yet to be born.

The Government's Euphemisms
June 13, 1995

There was nothing startlingly new about President Ezer Weizman's utterance yesterday on Israel's policy on the Golan. All he did was declare openly and clearly, as is his habit, what Foreign Minister Shimon Peres has said almost as explicitly and Prime Minister Yitzhak Rabin has hinted: Israel is willing to withdraw from the Golan to the international border, delineated by Mandatory powers Britain and France when the Golan was separated from Palestine and incorporated into French-ruled Syria in 1923.

What made Weizman's blunt statement news was that it came from him, the country's figurehead, rather than from the government. It is at least a year since the Syrian regime has been told by the U.S. mediators that Israel was ready to relinquish the whole Golan; and only a little less since every important government in the West and East, let alone all Arab dictators, has known of this Israeli concession.

Yet Israelis have been kept in the dark. With the kind of stubbornness one would like to see Israeli negotiators display at the negotiating table, Rabin has avoided telling the nation the complete truth. Clinging tenaciously to a honed formula, he has insisted that he will not "divulge" the line to which Israel is willing to retreat until other details of the agreement are ironed out.

To add insult to injury, government sources have implied that this deliberate vagueness is designed to keep the Syrians guessing. Nothing could be more ludicrous. After the Americans, Syrian President Hafez Assad was the first to know what Israel's intentions were.

Nor is the Golan issue the only area in which Israelis have been treated as children who should be kept in blissful ignorance for their own good. On a recent talk show on American television, hosted by Larry King, Rabin referred to the PLO-ruled area as a Palestinian state, quickly correcting himself to "Palestinian entity." And in France yesterday, he referred to "something less than a state." But no one in his audience either in Europe or in the U.S. treats these euphemisms seriously. All the European governments, as exemplified most recently by German Chancellor Helmut Kohl, treat the Arafat regime as a state. So does the UN. And they all assume that Israeli euphemisms are used strictly for internal consumption.

Inevitably, the consistent use of euphemisms shatters credibility. Rabin's cavalier way with the truth and his refusal to let Israelis in on a wide open secret can only cast doubt on his repeated vows on the indivisibility of Jerusalem. The PLO's announcement on Sunday that it would revive the old Jordanian-appointed municipality, which ceased functioning with the city's reunification in 1967, is a direct challenge to these vows.

Clearly, if two municipalities function in Jerusalem, declarations about the city's inviolability as Israel's capital will be taken as seriously as the government's pledges not to abandon the Golan and not to allow the establishment of a Palestinian state.

Appeasement on Jerusalem

June 22, 1995

In a surprise step, the Clinton administration has positioned itself squarely against Congress's intention to start building the American embassy in Jerusalem next year. Secretary of State Warren Christopher's letter warning Senate Majority Leader Robert Dole that a resolution calling for the embassy transfer would prompt a presidential veto seems aimed at stopping the bandwagon for the move. To date, 55 senators have signed on to the bill, initiated by Jon Kyl of Arizona and presented to the Senate on May 9 by Dole. Sixty-seven votes are needed to override a presidential veto.

Admitting that President Bill Clinton himself has promised to move the embassy - it was an explicit and unequivocal election pledge - Christopher rationalizes the threat of a veto by stating that nothing should be allowed to get in the way of the peace process in "an especially delicate period." Implying that Washington's credibility would be damaged if the bill passes, he states, "Few actions would be more explosive and harmful to these efforts than for the U.S., as the key sponsor of this process, to be pushing the Jerusalem issue forward." But it is disingenuous to suggest that a decision not to move the embassy will not be prejudicial. The reason the issue is "explosive" is that the PLO has threatened that it would "kill the process." To yield to this threat is to make every move the PLO dislikes hostage to the threat of "explosion." The proposed move of the U.S. embassy does not change the status of Jerusalem: the embassy is to be located in the western part of the city. But acquiescence to the demand not to move it at this time implies that even the fate of this part of Jerusalem is to be determined only in the final status negotiations with the PLO. It is not an impression the Clinton administration should be making.

Officials of AIPAC [American Israeli Political Action Committee], the "Jewish lobby" in Washington, have said that they will continue their efforts to sign up senators for the bill. They obviously feel that the move has the support of the vast majority of American Jews. Some Washington observers believe that the administration's move is only a ploy aimed at forcing a compromise on the bill, which they believe will be achieved before September.

But in threatening a veto, the message the administration must be heeding more than any other is Israel's thunderous silence. The subject of Jerusalem, on which the government is professing immovable determination, seems to have become an embarrassment. There is, to be sure, continuing lip service to the slogan "an undivided Jerusalem under Israeli sovereignty," but instead of giving the Dole bill the whole-hearted support it deserves, the government has been treating it as a piece of legislation about a remote town in Outer Mongolia.

The government has also been sending signals from Jerusalem itself which point to a less-than-total resoluteness. In an abject surrender to pressure from its Arab coalition partners and King Hussein, it has forfeited the right to expropriate land in Jerusalem. In another surrender - to naked violence - it has suspended the demolition of illegally built houses in the city. And, yielding to the familiar threats that the peace process would collapse if it took action, it has given tacit approval to the growing activities and rising profile of "Orient House" and other official Palestinian institutions in Jerusalem.

True, none of these surrenders have anything to do with Israel's sovereignty in western Jerusalem, which is what the move proposed in the Senate would recognize. But it is difficult to expect Washington to be more determined about resisting Arab threats on the Jerusalem issue than Israel seems

to be. One can only hope that the U.S. Senate will understand what the government has been unable to realize ever
since it signed the Oslo agreement: that no real peace can be
achieved through appeasement.

Olmert's Moment
June 26, 1995

If Mayor Ehud Olmert shuts down Orient House, as he
indicated over the weekend he would do, he will prove that
he belongs to that rare breed of politicians who keep their
campaign pledges. Not that he specifically committed himself to moving against Orient House during the election campaign. But one of his main promises to the voters, perhaps
the one which played a decisive role in helping him overcome Teddy Kollek's richly deserved popularity, was that he
would keep Jerusalem undivided and under Israeli sovereignty.
He kept reminding the electorate that while Kollek, too, is
nominally committed to the city's unification, the veteran
mayor's Labor affiliation and closeness to the government
militate against his defying the government's policies.

The existence of Orient House is a daily reminder that the
government's pledges on keeping the city united are about to
go the way of its other pre-election vows. Functioning as the
Palestinian Authority's foreign office, Orient House is only
one of more than 20 offices and agencies - ranging from the
office of agriculture to an investment and development authority to the energy research center - that function in Jerusalem on behalf of the Palestinian Authority. Their employees
get their salaries from the PA, their executives take their orders from the PA, and the world community, including the
Israeli government, recognizes them as offices of the PA. Even
the two offices the PA has promised to move out of the city -

the Palestinian Bureau of Statistics and the Communication office - are still in Jerusalem.

As *The Jerusalem Post* reported yesterday, Orient House has the kind of diplomatic immunity only embassies and consulates enjoy. Street rioters at the weekend knew that all they had to do to avoid arrest was to withdraw into the Orient House compound. They could continue to throw stones and bottles from there, and jeer at the impotent police, but they could not be detained. It is precisely this kind of status which Prime Minister Yitzhak Rabin once warned against. If the place starts functioning as a PLO foreign ministry, he said early last year, the whole peace process will be stopped.

Nor are the PA offices the only symptoms of creeping Palestinian sovereignty, and a parallel relinquishment of Israeli control, in the eastern part of the city. The Palestinian security services act freely among the city's Arab inhabitants (just as they do among the Arabs of Judea and Samaria); the PA has revived the Jordanian-appointed municipal council, dismissed by Israel in 1967, as the municipality of Arab inhabitants; and yesterday Foreign Minister Shimon Peres and Yasser Arafat agreed that Jerusalem's Arab residents will have the right to vote for the Palestinian national council. (The only matter still in dispute is whether they will have the right not only to elect but to be elected to the council, and whether the ballot boxes will be placed in the city or in neighboring towns.)

Olmert's authority is not on the political plane. As Peres said yesterday, he cannot make foreign policy decisions. But the law does empower him to enforce municipal regulations. If the operation of Orient House as a government building contradicts zoning laws, for example, there is no reason for the mayor to ignore the law and allow the operation to continue.

The government will undoubtedly fight the municipality

tooth and nail on this issue. But Olmert has the law on his side, and the support of a majority of Israelis. With bold, decisive action he can redeem an election pledge, save Jerusalem's unity, and enhance his credentials as a political leader.

Fire and Paralysis
July 3, 1995

In any other country, the results of a fire like the one which yesterday devastated a large area in the Jerusalem Corridor might have been considered relatively fortunate. After all, loss of life among both residents and firefighters is not un-common under such conditions. Yet yesterday no one was killed or gravely injured. And while property loss was exten-sive - at least 30 homes were destroyed and the harm to the environment is inestimable - it could have been much worse. Had the fire raged out of control during the night, the damage could have been immeasurably greater.

But Israel is not just any country. Even the most optimis-tic do not completely rule out the possibility of war or a ma-jor terrorist strike. And, clearly, the country cannot afford to be paralyzed by disaster, whether natural or man-made. The effects of such paralysis were driven home all too clearly when a power blackout recently shut down half the country. Yes-terday, too, traffic between Jerusalem and Tel Aviv came to a standstill for many hours, causing incalculable losses in time and money.

It will take a thorough investigation to determine the cause of the fire. It could have been arson, like the fire which de-stroyed much of the Mount Carmel forest six years ago, and the fact that the fire started in two separate locations is suspi-cious. But on the hottest day of the century it could have also been a spontaneous conflagration. Either way, the police and firefighters should have been prepared for the possibility of major fires on such hot, dry days, and once the fire began they should have foreseen the danger posed by high winds. Help should have arrived much faster, and the need to evacuate the affected areas recognized sooner.

Police Minister Moshe Shahal, who reached one of the worst-hit communities and witnessed several burning homes before the firefighters even arrived, said that the government should consider setting up a committee of inquiry. It is a good suggestion. But the committee should not devote its time merely to a postmortem; it should recommend emergency procedures to help prevent such disasters from affecting the life of the country. To expect the next calamity to end as benignly as yesterday's fire is nothing short of reckless.

The Continuing Battle

July 5, 1995

Ever since the Six Day War, Israel has tried to have its sovereignty over Jerusalem recognized by the world community, while establishing Jewish neighborhoods in the eastern part of the city to make unification irreversible.

The Arabs, too, have not been idle. Attempting to prevent what they call the "Judaization" of the city, they have moved in droves into the municipal boundaries, reversing the emigration trend during Jordanian rule. Their numbers in the city have increased at a faster rate than the Jewish population, and they have expanded the Arab neighborhoods dramatically, through legal and illegal building.

In recent years they also embarked on intensive political activity to restore Arab sovereignty in the city. As part of the Oslo agreement, they received official Israeli assurances that this activity could continue, and since then Orient House has become to all intents and purposes the Palestinian Authority's foreign ministry.

At one time Prime Minister Yitzhak Rabin asserted that continued political activity in Orient House would spell the end of the Oslo agreement. But the Palestinians not only ignored this threat - they opened 14 other offices which serve as government agencies under the direct control of the PA. They have even revived the Arab municipal council, dispersed in 1967. This move, clearly illegal, may have few practical applications, but it stressed the Palestinian disregard for the Oslo and Cairo agreements, which preclude changes in the political status quo in Jerusalem.

The government, particularly the Foreign Ministry, tries to minimize the importance of this activity. It routinely pretends that glaringly political talks at Orient House are no more than "courtesy calls," and it pooh-poohs the significance of other PA quasi-governmental offices in Jerusalem. Its attitude to the Jerusalem battle is ambiguous.

Worse, the Israel Police ignores the ubiquitous presence of the PA's secret police in the city, allowing Jibril Rajoub's Jericho-based Preventive Security operatives to act with impunity as a police force of a state within a state.

On Monday, Police Minister Moshe Shahal opposed a bill proposed by Yehoshua Matza (Likud) which would make "governmental or quasi-governmental activity" by Palestinians in Israel a criminal offense. Shahal insisted that it is virtually impossible to prove criminal intent in such cases, and that anyway the Gaza-Jericho Agreement Law already prohibits such activity. He has not explained why the police have done nothing to enforce this law.

It is difficult to blame the Palestinians for being unimpressed with the government's resolve. PLO officials have repeatedly promised Shahal that three of the PA offices - Statistics, Housing, and Information - will be moved out of Jerusalem, but the offices are still in the city. Yesterday, Peace Watch revealed that the PA has opened yet another office in Jerusalem - the Institute for the Palestinian Wounded, established by an order of PA Chairman Yasser Arafat to assist Palestinians injured in the intifada. As Peace Watch points out, there is no doubt that the institute is a PA agency. The PA is the source of its legal authority, its policies are set by the PA, and most of the funding is provided by the PA.

Clearly, the Palestinians have no intention of waiting for the final status talks to undermine Israel's hold in Jerusalem. To complement their creeping usurpation of authority in the eastern parts, they have recruited Israel's leading super-doves to support what they euphemistically call the "sharing" of Jerusalem. Having published advertisements to this effect, prominent peace camp activists, most of whom used to passionately support an undivided Jerusalem as Israel's eternal capital, yesterday joined Faisal Husseini in calling for "everybody's Jerusalem."

King Hussein, too, seems to have joined the battle. In an interview to an Italian paper he suggested dividing the city into three parts: a Palestinian capital, an Israeli capital, and an internationalized Old City. As former mayor Teddy Kollek has pointed out, a shared city is a political and technical impossibility. Jerusalem can either be divided into separate sovereignties, as it was before June 1967, or remain undivided under Israeli rule.

The only Israeli official who seems determined to combat this campaign to redivide Jerusalem is Mayor Ehud Olmert. On Monday he called a meeting with the police and justice ministers, Attorney-General Michael Ben-Yair, and other government officials. It resulted in a decision to press criminal charges against Faisal Husseini and other PLO officials in the city.

It must be hoped that Olmert will have both the courage and the power to press this battle and resist what is, at best, government indifference. With the help of some government ministers, apparently including Prime Minister Yitzhak Rabin, who still want all of Jerusalem to stay within Israel's borders, and with the support of what is still a broad public consensus, Olmert must lead the fight to keep the city undivided.

Security and Education

July 9, 1995

Stating in a *New York Times* interview on Friday that he had doubts about peace with the Palestinians, Prime Minister Yitzhak Rabin said most Israelis are "not convinced that the Palestinian Authority is capable or willing to cope with the terror."

What concerns most Israelis is how the Palestinians intend to use their growing power and authority. Even the most stringent and meticulous contracts are only as good as the intentions of their signatories - which is why Rabin, reflecting the wishes of a vast majority of Israelis, keeps insisting on the abolition of the offensive clauses in the PLO covenant. He wants to know that - at least formally - the Palestinians no longer aspire to destroy Israel and that they recognize its legitimacy.

But while the change in the charter is of great importance (if it is implemented - which is doubtful), it will prove useless unless the education of Arab children reflects the change. This is true of all Israel's neighbors, but particularly about the Palestinians. No one expects the Arab education system to treat Zionism lovingly, but it must reflect recognition of Israel as a legitimate fact of life in the Middle East.

Unfortunately, there is no sign of such a development.

On the contrary. Even today, no official school map anywhere in the Arab world, including Egypt and Jordan, contains the name Israel. And, incredibly, school curricula in the Arab schools in Judea- Samaria and Jerusalem are no better. To make matters worse, no Israeli government has ever done anything about this.

Recent articles in *Ma'ariv* and *Ha'aretz* expose a situation in Jerusalem's Arab schools which can only be described as shocking. What Arab students study in a city which is part of Israel's undivided capital is almost exactly what they study in Gaza and Nablus. Ever since the responsibility for education in the territories was transferred to the Palestinian Authority last August, the curriculum in Jerusalem's Arab schools has been controlled by the PA. Nor is it just a matter of the study materials. The symbols and trappings of the PA have been introduced to the schools as well.

This is true particularly in the private schools, run by church groups and other institutions. They receive only minimal support from the municipality, and they have always done whatever they wished. In several of these schools, PLO flags are raised as a matter of routine. The colors of the flag adorn the female students' dresses, and at a graduation last month, the Minister of Education was the guest of honor: not Amnon Rubinstein, but Yasser Amar, the PA's education minister.

The situation is not too different in the municipally run schools, supported by the Israeli taxpayer, to which half of Jerusalem's Arabs send their children. The study books and examination forms are adorned with the PA symbol, and Arafat's emissaries decide on appointments, resolve administrative and personal differences, and send instructions on how to run the schools. In these schools, too, the only maps are of pre-1948 Palestine, with the Jewish cities and villages omitted. Some of the teachers are convicted terrorists who were released in the disastrous "Jibril exchange" of 1985. It is not difficult to imagine what they tell their students about the Arab-Israeli conflict, particularly in the absence of textbooks on the subject.

Mayor Ehud Olmert became aware of this scandalous situation as soon as he took office. To correct it, he made larger appropriations than ever to the city's Arab schools, obtaining a special budget for the building of 180 new classrooms. He hoped not only to redress the budgetary inequality with the Jewish schools but to bring the Arab sector under greater Israeli influence.

But once the responsibility for Arab education in the territories was given to the PA, with the government failing to separate jurisdiction over Jerusalem from that of Judea-Samaria, he was outflanked. Bitterly, he told *Ma'ariv*, "This government is surrendering to the Palestinians in everything. In the sphere of land use, building, and of course education . . . I do whatever I can to stop their total takeover of education, but my authority is limited. All the keys are in the government's hands. It is they who must act."

Education Minister Amnon Rubinstein expressed shock at some of the findings. "I'll meet with the mayor to ensure that schools we subsidize do not have Palestinian trappings. It will be very difficult, but we have to tell the teachers and principals, 'Choose. If you are financed by us you cannot belong to the Palestinian Authority.' . . . As far as I am concerned using a map in which Israel does not appear is an anti-Israel act of hostility. A map of this sort also contravenes the agreement on the transfer of authority."

But in the current atmosphere, it is doubtful that anything will be done. The proper solution is to introduce the curriculum of the Israeli Arab schools in Jerusalem's Arab schools. This was tried after the 1967 war, but Arab protests made the government back down. Now the prevailing feeling is that any attempt to sever the connection between the schools and the PA will cause a storm which the government will be unable and unwilling to weather.

What the Palestinians understand, and the government fails to comprehend, is that as long as they can keep educating their children to think of Israel as a temporary, illegitimate phenomenon, there will be no real peace and certainly no integration and coexistence. It is this, even more than the immediate security threat, that should give the government pause.

More Orient House Scandals
July 18, 1995

After visiting Orient House on Saturday, Austrian Secretary of State for Foreign Affairs Benita Ferroro-Waldner said she intended to meet no Israeli officials, because she did not want to disturb their Sabbath. It was a classic example of an excuse being worse than the act which begat it. The schedule of the Austrian deputy to the foreign minister must be harrowingly crowded, perhaps even more crowded than that of the U.S. secretary of state, but it is somehow difficult to imagine that she could not spend more than precisely 25 hours in Jerusalem. Nor could her sneering remark be mistaken for anything other than the disingenuous, patronizing, and contemptuous attitude characteristic of pre-1945 Austrian officials.

If anything topped this hypocritical diplomatic charade it was the reaction of our own Foreign Ministry. Providing a superb example of man's infinite capacity for diagnosing spit as rain, it expressed relief that the Austrian diplomat saved it an embarrassment by not requesting a meeting with Israeli officials after paying an official visit to Orient House. It seems that by Foreign Ministry criteria there is nothing wrong with treating Orient House as the seat of the Palestinian government and calling for the establishment of a Palestinian capital in the city, as long as the existence of the Israeli sovereignty in the neighborhood is ignored.

Just as disturbing is the story of another recent incident at Orient House. The Border Police unit stationed opposite the compound stopped what it considered a suspicious car entering the gate two weeks ago. Orient House officials emerged and demanded their release, but since they refused to identify themselves, the police rejected the request. Faisal Husseini then called the Police Ministry on his cellular phone, and the police commander was ordered by ministry adviser Moshe Sasson to relent.

Soon after, Palestinian officials demanded that the police remove an Israeli flag they had raised at their post. When the police refused, Husseini intervened again, and again a high ministry official ordered the unit commander to do as Husseini had requested. The Israeli flag was promptly removed.

The emerging picture is all too clear. Despite its repeated vows to stop the political and diplomatic activities of Orient House, and despite Prime Minister Yitzhak Rabin's warning that the peace process would be halted if such activities continue, the government is accepting the encroachment of Palestinian sovereignty in Jerusalem with perfect equanimity.

Nor is the government going to let anyone else do anything about this encroachment. Mayor Ehud Olmert's efforts to use city ordinances to stop Orient House violations of zoning laws is being effectively frustrated by Attorney-General Michael Ben-Yair. Claiming that Olmert is acting out of political motives rather than purely municipal concerns, Ben-Yair issued an opinion last week opposing Olmert's actions. One wonders what he would have said when the U.S. convicted the famous gangster Al Capone, not for the many violent crimes he had committed, but for income tax evasion.

Secret Agreements on Jerusalem
July 21, 1995

The most disturbing aspect of the recent arrests of 11 Palestinian Authority operatives in Jerusalem is that it has taken the Police Ministry so long to acknowledge their activities. Turning a blind eye to Palestinian efforts to establish a state within a state in Jerusalem is bad enough; misleading the public with assertions that no such efforts are being made is worse.

Yesterday's announcement of the arrests confirmed what has been widely known: that under the noses of the Israeli police in Jerusalem there is a whole structure of Palestinian Mafia-like enforcers who operate with virtual impunity. A Palestinian "police station," discovered yesterday in the Arab village of Issawiya, is but one example of their entrenchment.

These police are no different from security forces in the Arab dictatorships. They routinely beat suspects, demand bribes, collect protection money and mete out justice without the benefit of law courts. Their kidnapped victims are tortured, sometimes to death, in Jericho prisons. And the protection money they receive from Arab merchants, hotel owners and business offices in Jerusalem goes to the PA treasury.

Prime Minister Yitzhak Rabin recently stated that over 200 such Palestinian security agents operate in eastern Jerusalem. More realistic estimates put the number at 400. They are all on the payroll of the Jericho Preventive Security apparatus, financed by well-meaning donor countries. The force is headed by Arafat's confidant Jibril Rajoub, a leading Fatah terrorist and a veteran of Israeli prisons who is the undisputed boss of the Arab population in Judea and Samaria. He is also one of the leading Palestinian delegates at the current "second stage" negotiations in Zichron Ya'acov.

The actions of the Palestinian Police in Jerusalem are only one part of the attempt to tear the city's Arab population away from Israeli control. Rajoub's agents also purchase land in Jerusalem for the PA, in violation of the agreement which prohibits PA activity in Jerusalem. There is even an effort afoot to acquire the land intended for the American Embassy in the city.

Yesterday yet another revelation was made: that a secret agreement, signed in Cairo on June 21 by the head of Israel's civil administration, Brig.-Gen. David Shahaf and deputy PA Finance Minister Atef Alawneh stipulates that Arab taxpayers and businesses in eastern Jerusalem can pay their income taxes and VAT directly to the PA. (This, one assumes, is in addition to the protection money.)

That the agreement has been a secret is as dismaying as it is suspicious. Kept under wraps by the government until it was exposed by the organization Shalom LeDorot (Peace for Generations), the agreement actually includes a conspiratorial provision: "It is concluded with Dr. Alawneh that these oral agreements will be executed in letter and in spirit. For the good of the cause, however, publicizing the agreements and giving them political meaning should be avoided. . . ."

Mayor Ehud Olmert's assertion yesterday that keeping such an agreement secret "was intended to mislead the people and conceal the grave implications of the arrangement" can hardly be disputed. The implications are clear: the agreement legitimates the administrative (if not yet political) splitting of Jerusalem.

Nor is this the first secret pact which affects Jerusalem's future. As revealed recently by Peace Watch, a secret agreement was signed in Rome in January 1994 between then-head of the General Security Service Ya'acov Perry and then-deputy chief of the general staff Amnon Shahak on the Israeli side, and Rajoub and Mohammed Dahlan on the Palestinian side.

It provided that the PA's Preventive Security police will have freedom of action throughout Judea and Samaria, not only in the self-rule areas. This, combined with the assurance that such PA institutions as the Orient House and other ministerial offices could continue functioning in Jerusalem, made the extension of Palestinian Police activities into Jerusalem a natural step.

The PA cannot, then, be faulted for trying to consolidate its power and control among the city's 150,000 Arabs. The government has not only done nothing to discourage separation in the city, it has acted to accelerate it.

The very fact that Israel has agreed to allow Jerusalem Arabs to vote for the Palestinian legislative council and even be elected to it is tantamount to relinquishing its authority over the city's Arab inhabitants. (True, candidates for the council may have to have a nominal second residence outside city limits, but this hardly fools anyone.) That Jerusalem Arabs can now pay taxes directly to the PA makes the division complete.

Rabin and some of his ministers still routinely repeat the mantra that Jerusalem will remain the undivided capital of Israel. But the government's actions point to an acquiescence in the division of the city. In every speech Yasser Arafat makes, he declares that Jerusalem will be the capital of the Palestinian state. He may know whereof he speaks.

Yielding on the Temple Mount
August 7, 1995

To those who lived in this country during the British Mandate, yesterday's scenes at the Temple Mount must have seemed like a case of deja vu. Jewish worshippers, attempting to exercise a court-approved right to pray on the Temple Mount, went to the site expecting police protection. Forewarned of likely Arab objections, 1,800 police were assembled there, ready to enforce the law. But when some Arabs, a hundred at the most, threatened to riot, it was the Jews who were forcibly hauled off and deprived of the right to pray in the area.

To explain their conduct, the police seemed to use a verbatim copy of British announcements in the 1930s. The danger of disturbances was real, they said, and the consequences of allowing the Jews to pray unknown. To prevent the disruption of public order, the gates of the Mount were shut to all worshippers, Jews and Moslems alike. The prohibition on prayer was unfortunate, they said, but it was intended to forestall a disturbance.

Not unlike the British explanations of six decades ago, this police communique contained regrettable inaccuracies. Yesterday's ban on Jews was indeed total, but a few hundred Moslems did pray on the Mount. The police said there were 400 of them. According to Likud MK David Mena they numbered 1,000. But it is not the numbers that matter. The fact is that the doors were closed only to Jews.

Nor would there have been any equality of treatment had both Moslems and Jews been prevented from praying yesterday. The court-ordered permission for Jews applied only to Tisha Be'Av, [a fast day which commemorates] the day the Temple on this site was destroyed. The Moslems can pray on the Mount any time. (Letting the Moslem religious establishment prohibit all but Moslem worshippers on the Temple Mount's open field is one of Israel's most puzzling concessions.)

Perhaps most indicative of what led to yesterday's events was the urgent call on Moslems to converge on the Mount to prevent Jews from worshipping there. The appeal was made not only in Jerusalem mosques, but - in flagrant violation of the Cairo agreement - by Yasser Arafat and Faisal Husseini.

The Arabs heeded this call, and when the first Jews were

allowed on the Mount in the morning, the small Arab mob menaced them. Hearing that the worshippers were being threatened, the police commander, coordinating activities from another area, angrily said, "We are in control here, we will not be told what to do by anyone." But within minutes he yielded to the Wakf [Moslem religious council] and Husseini and withdrew the Jews from the Mount.

It is entirely possible that had the police insisted on enforcing the law by letting Jews pray on the Mount, the Arabs would have rioted. But if threats of Arab rioting had been allowed to deter Jews in this country, there would have been no Israel. And if there is one lesson to be learned from past experience, it is that surrender to threats brings only temporary calm. In the long run, it guarantees increase of appetite, escalation of aggression, and bloodshed.

Contest of Wills over Jerusalem
August 15, 1995

The debate in and out of the government over Orient House tends to obscure a plain fact: Orient House operates as the foreign ministry of the Palestinian Authority and is recognized as such throughout the world.

Nominally, Farouk Kadoumi, who opposes the Oslo agreements, is the PLO's foreign minister. But he has been used by Yasser Arafat mostly as a roving ambassador to Islamic countries and has yet to set foot in the self-rule areas. The Palestinian Authority minister who occupies a position second only to Arafat's, and with whom foreign dignitaries meet as a matter of routine, is Faisal Husseini. Not by accident, he also wears the hat of PA minister for Jerusalem, and he meets visiting dignitaries only in Jerusalem, at Orient House.

The activity at Orient House would not shame the chancery of any power. As the non-partisan organization Peace Watch revealed yesterday, in the 15 months since the signing of the Cairo agreement on May 4, 1994, representatives of 29 countries have held 50 diplomatic meetings at Orient House. These representatives - from Russia, Germany, France, Canada, Egypt, Austria, Spain, Sweden, Ireland, Holland, India, and Turkey among others - have included one prime minister, two deputy prime ministers, five foreign ministers, two deputy foreign ministers, and nine other ministers. According to Article 5 of Annex II to the Declaration of Principles, repeated in the Cairo agreement, the offices of the Palestinian Authority must be located only in Gaza and Jericho.

Orient House is not the only PA institution in Jerusalem. Peace Watch mentions eight agencies directly under the PA, and two others linked to the PA. But if all national Palestinian institutions - including the PLO youth club and the national theater - are counted, the number of Palestinian governmental offices in Jerusalem reaches 38.

No great insight is required to understand the reason for this proliferation. As Arafat says in every speech, the PLO's goal is to establish Jerusalem as the capital of the Palestinian state, and "to plant the Palestinian flag on the minarets and churches of Jerusalem." What he is doing now is establishing "facts on the ground."

Moreover, he has good reason to believe that he has the support of at least part of the Israeli government. In a letter (whose existence he first denied, then admitted to the Knesset) to Norwegian Foreign Minister Johan Jorgen Holst on the issue of Jerusalem, Foreign Minister Shimon Peres wrote in October 1993 that "the Palestinian institutions of East Jerusalem . . . are of great importance and will be preserved."

Though in a recent letter to Peace Watch Peres insists that these institutions were meant to be "non-governing," he has expressed support for formal visits of foreign emissaries at

Orient House. He now insists that Sweden's Deputy Prime Minister Muna Salin be allowed to confer with Husseini at Orient House during her forthcoming visit to Israel. In fact, he has already approved her visit to Husseini, which he describes as a 10-minute courtesy call.

Peres's policies are not wholly compatible with Prime Minister Yitzhak Rabin's insistence that the one concession Israel will never make is on Jerusalem's indivisibility. Rabin has encouraged Police Minister Moshe Shahal to act against visits by foreign officials to Orient House on the pretext that they may cause public unrest. He has backed Mayor Ehud Olmert's plans to act against Orient House on the municipal level. And he has approved Olmert's moves against members of the Arab "municipal council" - a body appointed by Jordan before 1967 and recently revived and financed by Arafat - who illegally represent themselves as the municipal government of "Arab Jerusalem."

Peres must realize that no final status agreement with the Palestinians can be reached without conceding eastern Jerusalem. He probably hopes that, as the visits to Orient House become routine, Israelis will get used to the presence of the Palestinian institutions and flag in Jerusalem. Rabin, on the other hand, still seems to hope that a division of the city can be avoided.

What seems to be looming is another contest of wills between the two Labor leaders. But if recent history is any indication, this one, too, will be won by Peres. After all, it was only a year ago that Rabin emphatically announced that if Orient House ever served as the PA's foreign ministry, the whole peace process would be halted.

Toughness, Sensible and Otherwise
August 18, 1995

In both words and deeds, the government has been displaying unusual toughness over the past few days. Some of it has been directed not at the country's adversaries but at the residents of Judea and Samaria. Speaking to a United Jewish Appeal mission on Wednesday, Prime Minister Yitzhak Rabin made what can only be described as gratuitous, provocative remarks about the "settlers," implying that they are parasites. "Who needs them?" he said, "they don't do anything for us."

It is not the first time Rabin has referred to the residents of the territories as a security burden and an egregious financial liability. But with deep existential anxiety sweeping these communities at the prospect of "Oslo 2," such language ensures the escalation of internal tensions.

Hearing such demonization of the "settlers" from the premier, law enforcement agencies - particularly the police under Police Minister Moshe Shahal - can hardly be expected to conduct themselves as required by law, let alone civilly, when confronting anti-government demonstrations. Indeed, indiscriminate police brutality and cases of wanton cruelty have reached an unprecedented and frightening level.

It is difficult to imagine what prompts Rabin to so rudely and mindlessly malign 150,000 people who enjoy the support of more than half the country's Jewish population. Some Rabin advisers claim that his blunt, barracks language gains him popularity. But surely he must realize that if there is one thing common to virtually the whole nation today, it is the fear of civil strife. A vast majority, including many of his dedicated supporters, must deem the use of inflammatory, hate-filled rhetoric at a time like this irresponsible and unacceptable.

But Rabin has also shown some toughness where it makes

sense. Yesterday, having received a green light from the prime minister's office, the police entered some of the Palestinian offices in Jerusalem to investigate their connections with the Palestinian Authority.

It is an investigation long overdue. As Peace Watch has shown, the connections with the PA of at least 10 of these Jerusalem agencies are illegal. Acting as governmental ministries, they are in flagrant violation of the Oslo and Cairo agreements, which restrict all government activity to the self-rule areas.

The ultimate target of these investigations is clearly Orient House. Foreign Minister Shimon Peres and Economics Minister Yossi Beilin have expressed fear that shutting down Orient House would cause a diplomatic storm. But the continued presence in the heart of Jerusalem of this Palestinian foreign ministry, recognized as such by much of the world, makes a mockery of the government's pledge to keep Jerusalem undivided under Israeli sovereignty.

The government would obviously prefer to postpone the fight over Jerusalem, but the first battle has already been joined. And letting the PA maintain and enlarge its foothold in the city can only ensure Israel's defeat. Efforts to dislodge an even more entrenched Orient House at a later date will trigger not only worldwide protest but insurmountable resistance both here and abroad.

That the government has decided to move against the PA in Jerusalem may indicate that it is becoming aware of growing popular doubts about the Oslo agreement. It is an awareness which may be reflected in the Peres interview in today's *Jerusalem Post*.

Having referred, intentionally or otherwise, to a "Palestinian state," Peres has been considered the most dedicated government advocate of Palestinian sovereignty on the 1949 armistice lines. Now he maintains that "the West Bank may remain without sovereignty," and that the Jewish residents of the territories will "remain Israeli citizens forever." (Unlike Rabin, Peres is far too judicious in his choice of words to vilify these communities, some of which he helped establish.)

But Peres's tough-sounding musings are not matched by a realistic political approach. To envision a territory without sovereignty after the expectations for a Palestinian state have been raised not only among Arabs but throughout the world is to indulge in wishful thinking. Once Israel forfeits military control, nothing can prevent Yasser Arafat from declaring a state and receive world recognition for it. He has a staff working on the declaration right now.

Nor is it easy to understand Peres's dismissal of Arafat's intentions, exposed in recent speeches, as irrelevant because of Israel's overwhelming power. Recent history has made it amply clear that terrorism is not a function of power, yet it can make the life of the most powerful miserable if not unbearable. Nor is the power arrayed against Israel limited to the Palestinian terror groups. The territorial concessions to the PLO endanger Israel because they can be used by other Arab regimes, not just the Palestinians.

Yet there is one promising thought forwarded by Peres. It is the idea that the "settlers" can continue being Israeli citizens even if they are not under Israeli sovereignty. By the same token, the Arab inhabitants of the territories can have Jordanian citizenship while living under Israeli sovereignty. As citizens of another state, they will not threaten Israel with becoming a bi-national state. And, as Rabin told the UJA [United Jewish Appeal] group on Wednesday, it is only this threat which has prompted Israel's decision to withdraw from Judea and Samaria.

Talks and Bombs Combination
August 22, 1995

President Ezer Weizman seemed shaken yesterday when the crowd at the site of the bus bombing in Jerusalem's Ramot Eshkol refused to listen to him. He must have assumed, not unreasonably, that he is popular even among the most hawkish opponents of the negotiations, and that any crowd, no matter how agitated, would let him speak. He is, after all, the only public figure in office who has called for at least a temporary suspension of the talks.

Angered by the crowd's lack of appreciation for his presence, Weizman walked away. Although far more attuned to public feelings than the government, he seems to underestimate the frustration and bitterness which torment a majority of the country's Jewish population. Nor does he seem to realize what it is that the public so resents.

Obviously, terrorist acts which kill men, women, and children in the center of Jewish cities in what is supposed to be the dawn of a new era of peace have a demoralizing effect. Since the signing of the Oslo agreement, 150 Israelis have been killed by terrorists, 98 of them since Yasser Arafat took over in Gaza and Jericho. This is a much larger number than in any similar period since the establishment of the state.

But the Israeli public is no stranger to terrorism, and it would have been able to cope with the carnage with greater fortitude had its painful injuries not been compounded with egregious insults. The most obvious offenses are the gratuitous epithets Prime Minister Yitzhak Rabin seems to enjoy flinging at anyone - including members of his own party - who registers the slightest reservation about his policies. Worse, he tends to blame everyone in sight for his failures.

Even yesterday, only hours after the bus bombing, he managed to imply that it is the anti-government demonstrations which keep police forces from effectively fighting terrorists. In fact, no democratic government in recent history has devoted such large forces to suppress peaceful protests.

As if to prove this, a news broadcast immediately following Rabin's press conference yesterday reported that, at a peaceful demonstration in Tel Aviv, the number of police was as large as that of the protesters. With such a disproportionate deployment of the security forces, often against women and the elderly, the public can hardly be blamed for believing that the government's dedication to discouraging dissent is far too high on its order of priorities.

The public must also find it difficult to digest the government's strenuous efforts to rehabilitate and lionize Yasser Arafat. Rabin made a point of stressing that the Palestinian Authority not only combats terrorism in Gaza, but collaborates with Israel in fighting Hamas and Islamic Jihad in Judea and Samaria.

But the fact is that the collaboration is extremely limited, and its results - according to intelligence sources - quite insignificant. The Palestinian security services' long chase after the Hamas operative in Gaza who was allegedly planning a car bombing in Israel, followed by a promise to immediately release him, only confirmed the public's suspicions that the Palestinian war on terror is nothing but a charade.

The government is so eager to exonerate Arafat of any connection with terrorism that it persistently points to organizations abroad as the initiators of the recent bombings. But the public must sense that Arafat's speeches calling for jihad, praising the "martyrs" who fall in the struggle against Israel and comparing the Oslo agreement to Mohammed's treaty with the tribe of Koreish are incompatible with his condemnations of terrorism. [The treaty with Koreish was made for expedience with the intention to break it as soon as conquest was possible.]

Yesterday, the Hamas broadcast from Syria not only refrained from attacking Arafat; it called for Arafat's political activity to continue simultaneously with Hamas's armed struggle, so that Israel's departure from the territories would be assured. As television commentator Ehud Ya'ari put it, this is an accurate reflection of reality. Indeed, the results of combining talks with bombings seems to work well for the Palestinians. The government has made it clear that, if anything, terrorist strikes will only prompt it to accelerate the "process" and the army's withdrawal.

Yet despite all this, it is highly likely that the public would support the process if only it saw a light at the end of the tunnel. There are, after all, few motivators more powerful than hope for a brighter future. If such hope seems absent today, it is because even government spokesmen find it difficult to promise the cessation of terrorism. Most of the Jewish population in this country seems to believe that, if anything, the relinquishment of control over Judea and Samaria means only that the terrorists will be able to operate more freely and efficiently from new bases.

Foreign Minister Shimon Peres said yesterday that the fight against terrorism can only succeed if its root causes - by which he means the "occupation" - are removed. Surely he must realize by now that, to the terrorists, not only an IDF [Israeli Defense Force] checkpost in Jenin represents an occupation, but the presence of an Israeli bus in Ramot Eshkol.

Close PA's Jerusalem Offices
August 29, 1995

The most troublesome aspect of the Palestinian Authority's operations in Jerusalem is the subterfuge it has used. Aware that governmental activities outside the self-rule areas are prohibited in the Oslo and the Cairo agreements, the PA keeps insisting that they are not what they seem to be, that the authority's Jerusalem offices are nothing but local service agencies. But the police and the General Security Service have established that this is plainly false. And the evidence presented by Peace Watch, which monitors compliance with the Oslo agreement, points to the simple fact that these offices are nothing but PA ministries.

Perhaps most indicative of the deception the PA practices is that the three offices now ordered closed by the police were supposed to move out of Jerusalem months ago. The Palestinian Bureau of Statistics (PBS), for example, had agreed to move to Ramallah. In fact, in a letter dated July 13 to Knesset Interior Committee Chairman Yehoshua Matza, Police Minister Moshe Shahal actually asserted that the PBS was no longer operating in Jerusalem, having moved to the Al Rian building in Ramallah. But the office continued to function without the slightest change in its routine. Even the sign outside the building identifying the PBS office as such is still in place.

That the police minister could convey such false information to a Knesset member is regrettable. It seems to affirm the suspicion that in its dealings with the PLO the government's gullibility is infinite, and its inability to acknowledge facts which get in the way of its perceptions is total.

Nor are the three offices being shut down by the police the only such ministries operating in Jerusalem. Peace Watch has identified at least seven other governmental offices directly linked to the PA, and two more whose links are not clear. At the head of the line is Orient House, which serves as the PA's foreign ministry. Far more than any other Palestinian institution in the city, it represents a challenge to Israel's sovereignty.

To counter the Israeli move, Palestinian leaders have issued the by-now-familiar threats that closing the offices would precipitate unrest in Jerusalem and torpedo the talks. As the government may have noticed by now, it is a hollow threat. No one needs progress in the talks more than the Palestinians, and except for some token suspension of official meetings between the negotiators, the talks will undoubtedly go on.

What both sides understand is that the move this week against the three Jerusalem offices is a preliminary test of wills in the battle for the city. If Israel backs down, Orient House will not only continue to function with impunity; its activities will become more ostentatious than ever. But if Israel ignores the Palestinian protests and threats, and refuses to allow a threatened Palestinian court challenge to delay the implementation of the evacuation order, its credibility will be enhanced, and it may be able to muster enough courage to close Orient House as well. The government's resolve in this confrontation will say much about its announced determination to keep Jerusalem undivided under Israeli sovereignty.

Capitulation in Jerusalem

September 3, 1995

Last week, Police Minister Moshe Shahal announced with great flourish that three of the seven major governmental offices run by the PA in Jerusalem had been presented with an ultimatum: either close down or be shut down by the police.

The reason for the Israeli demand was obvious: the activities of all Palestinian offices in Jerusalem - which include seven PA ministries and 30 other public institutions connected with the PA - violate the Oslo and Cairo agreements. According to these agreements, all PA activity must be confined to Gaza and Jericho. The existence of these offices in Jerusalem is an infringement on Israeli sovereignty, and an illegal attempt to establish "facts on the ground" in Jerusalem before the final-status talks begin.

But these stipulations in the agreements Israel has signed with the PLO are contradicted by a commitment made by Foreign Minister Shimon Peres. In a letter to the late Norwegian foreign minister Johan Jorgen Holst, Peres obligated Israel to allow Palestinian offices and institutions in Jerusalem to continue functioning. That this letter was kept secret until boastfully revealed by Arafat, and that Peres initially denied its existence to the Knesset seems to indicate that Peres knew it would be difficult to reconcile its contents with the Declaration of Principles.

Now these conflicting obligations are coming home to roost. In what can only be viewed as a capitulation, Shahal agreed on Thursday that the three offices (the Palestinian Health Council, Broadcasting Corporation and Statistics Center) may remain in Jerusalem provided they sign declarations "affirming they are not connected with the Palestinian Authority."

To treat such declarations more seriously than Arafat's solemn pledge of September 9, 1993 to abolish the Palestinian Covenant is to give gullibility a bad name. Obviously, these institutions have not the slightest intention to sever themselves from the PA. And while they may, to let Shahal save face, make some changes in bookkeeping procedures, they will continue to receive funding from the PA, directly or circuitously, and follow Yasser Arafat's instructions to the letter.

The attempt to close the three offices was clearly a test of wills. Had Shahal stood his ground, the other offices would have also been closed. Even Orient House itself - the PA's foreign ministry in the heart of Jerusalem - might have been transferred to Gaza. Now that Israel has retreated, the opposite will happen: the Palestinian offices will operate with even greater freedom, strengthened by a successful baptism by fire. Parallel to Shahal's ignominious retreat, Justice Minister David Liba'i met with Jerusalem PLO official Faisal Husseini and lectured him on the need to obey Israeli law and terminate PA activities in Orient House. Husseini came out of the meeting confessing that such activities have indeed taken place at Orient House (something he used to deny with vehement indignation) but, he said, these have been stopped and only activities compatible with the Oslo and Cairo agreements now take place there.

As if to ensure that such promises are not taken too seriously, Husseini called for a general meeting of Palestinian leaders and PA functionaries at Orient House to discuss the future of Palestinian institutions and protest Israel's efforts to limit its activities. They called on Arab countries to aid the institutions and help protect them against what they called "harassment by Jewish settlers who have been campaigning for their closure." For good measure they also called for a boycott of the Jerusalem 3000 celebrations.

The government's dilemma is as real as it is unenviable. Having signed agreements on the one hand and a letter which contradicts them on the other, it cannot prevent Palestinian encroachment on Israel's sovereignty in Jerusalem. Both sides realize that the confrontation over these offices are but the first salvos in the battle for Jerusalem. And the opinion polls which show that 63 percent of the Arab residents of Jerusalem prefer war to having Israel continue to "occupy" the eastern part of the city must make them understand that the battle will be long and difficult.

Mayor Ehud Olmert, who said on Thursday "The government has taken one step forward and two steps back," would clearly like to shut down these institutions, for fear that otherwise Israel may lose the first round in the fight for sovereignty, but it is doubtful that he has the authority to do so. It is likely that Prime Minister Yitzhak Rabin, who has backed Olmert on this issue, would also want to eliminate these daily insults to Israel's rule in Jerusalem. But only a reckless gambler would venture a bet on the ability of the nation's prime minister and the capital's mayor to reverse the concessionary course the government has chosen to take.

Jerusalem, Still to be Won
September 5, 1995

That Christianity and Islam consider Jerusalem a holy city may be viewed by Jews as a form of flattery. It is only because they tried to compete with the Jewish religion and supersede it that they claimed Jerusalem as their own. The city, now routinely described as holy to the three great monotheistic religions, would have meant nothing at all had it not been central to Judaism and the capital of the Jewish nation.

Yet Jews cannot and must not forget that there is a world of difference between what Jerusalem means to them and the role the city plays in Christianity and Islam. There is nothing in the annals of mankind like the relationship between the Jewish nation and Jerusalem.

This is not only because for 3,000 years Jews have considered Jerusalem their spiritual capital and faced Jerusalem in prayer. Nor only because there is no equivalent in history to the vow "next year in Jerusalem," made by Jews everywhere with tenacious, heart-rending consistency for two millennia. Nor is it just because there is no other capital and holy place for Jews.

Above all, Jerusalem is unique because it is the apotheosis of the dream of return, the quintessence of the vision of rebirth which has kept the Jewish nation alive since the destruction of the Temple. Prime Minister Yitzhak Rabin put it aptly when, opening the celebrations of Jerusalem's 3,000th birthday yesterday at the Knesset, he said, "There is no Israel without Jerusalem, and there is no peace without undivided Jerusalem, the City of Peace."

Appropriately, he also quoted David Ben-Gurion's statement on the occasion of the move of Israel's government offices to the capital in 1949: "The State of Israel has always had and will always have only one capital, eternal Jerusalem. This is how it was 3,000 years ago, and this is how we believe it will be for eternity." The city is not only a physical capital. It is "the heart of the Jewish people," he stressed. Indeed, to deny Jerusalem's centrality in Jewish life and its role as the Jewish capital is to deny Jews their most fundamental rights as a nation.

Other claims to the city are dwarfed by these facts of history. To strenuously point to Roman and Ottoman architecture or pre-Israelite artifacts found in Jerusalem as proof of the city's universality and diversity, and to suggest that the celebration should commemorate all its inhabitants, beginning with the Canaanites and Jebusites, is an insult to history and common sense - a laughable, self-deprecating bow to politically correct multi-culturalism.

For all but Jews, Jerusalem has never been anything but just another town. Except for the short-lived Crusader kingdom, no other nation has ever made the city its capital. In fact, all non-Jews have treated it as occupiers, making a special effort to destroy its Jewish character and limit, if not eliminate, freedom of worship for any religion but their own.

One way or another, they tried to emulate the Romans, who attempted to erase Jerusalem's Jewish identity by changing its name to Aelia Capitolina. To suggest now that the city be divided again, that half of it become a capital of a Palestinian state, or that parts of it be internationalized, is to attempt such erasure by other means.

It would have been nice had the celebrations of Jerusalem's 3,000th anniversary coincided with world recognition of the city as Israel's undivided capital. That no such recognition is imminent was clearly demonstrated by the absence of the American and European ambassadors at the opening celebrations of the city's birthday.

That the European nations have decided, with typical nasty pettiness and plain malice, to boycott the celebrations is yet another indication that the days of the double standard are far from over. There is no other nation on earth whose capital is not recognized as such by the vast majority of the world community. Unfortunately, Jerusalem is also unique in that no Israeli government has made the recognition of the capital by the major powers topmost in its order of priorities.

Rabin concluded his speech by asserting that "undivided Jerusalem is ours. Jerusalem forever." But no one is more aware than the premier that the battle for Jerusalem has only just begun, and that in the first skirmishes Israel has by no means been the victor.

Israel has capitulated on its demand that three Palestinian Authority governmental offices in the city be shut down. In its update on the encroachment of the PA on Jerusalem, Peace Watch yesterday revealed that there are now 11 major offices in the city connected to the PA, as opposed to seven listed six months ago. And despite Rabin's vow to put an end to the illegal operations of Orient House, there is no indication that the government intends to do anything about it.

The year of celebrations begun yesterday is intended to

highlight the uniqueness of the 3,000 year bond of the Jewish people to Jerusalem. If it also reminds Jews in Israel and the Diaspora [all areas outside of Israel] that the battle for Jerusalem is yet to be won, it will have served its purpose.

Indyk's Absence
September 6, 1995

If there is one thing Israelis neither need nor want from an American ambassador it is to have their intelligence insulted. For Ambassador Martin Indyk to say, as he did yesterday, that he had snubbed the opening celebrations of Jerusalem's 3,000th birthday because of a previous engagement is to give the white lies of diplomacy a bad name. To use this excuse after initially claiming that the event was "cultural" and therefore warranted only the presence of the cultural attaché is to add insult to injury.

The reason Indyk did not attend the celebration is as plain as it is obvious: the Clinton administration decided that it would not be in the U.S. interest to do so. Washington has a perfect right to assume that its ambassador's appearance at the Israeli celebrations in Jerusalem would compromise its position as an "honest broker" in the Israel-Arab negotiations, and it is its prerogative to draw the appropriate conclusions from this assumption. But if the U.S. really considers Israel a friend and an ally, it should spare it the patronizing excuses.

The government, too, must draw the proper conclusions from the incident. Letting the press know Prime Minister Yitzhak Rabin was miffed and upset may help alleviate anger and frustration, but it fails to address a very real problem.

The Clinton administration may be the friendliest since the establishment of the state, but like previous administrations it is wedded to the notion that Israel must withdraw to the 1949 armistice lines with minor border changes. What makes it different is that it believes Israel can be cajoled, rather than pressured, into withdrawing - a belief the current government has done nothing to dispel.

The administration also assumes that such an Israeli withdrawal can be achieved only if Israel feels strong and secure. To enhance this feeling, it has pursued a policy of unprecedented military cooperation and diplomatic support. But it pursues traditional American dogma in aspiring to a Pax Americana in the region, in which Israel will be a protectorate, depending on American backing and sponsorship, rather than on strategic depth and topographic advantage for its defense. It is a concept which not only contradicts Zionist ideals of self-sufficiency and independence, but which has proved disastrous in the past four decades.

Israel has hoped that on the issue of Jerusalem, Bill Clinton is committed to his campaign pledge of June 14, 1992: "I recognize Jerusalem as an undivided city and the eternal capital of Israel." Monday's incident put this in doubt. It could be, of course, that the administration simply meant to keep a "neutral" stance now, and that it intends to support Israel's position once the Jerusalem question comes up in the final-status talks. But it is far more likely that Washington will seek a "compromise" that will divide the city into Israeli and Palestinian halves.

Aware of the nature of the problem, Economics Minister Yossi Beilin said yesterday that the incident constituted a "moment of truth," which signaled that the status quo was unacceptable.

"What happened was a shocking truth for many people who think that what we need to do . . . is to leave the situation in Jerusalem as it is," he said. "We need to come to a situation where in the final arrangement the world will recognize Jerusalem as our capital." What Beilin means by a changed situation is clear: if Israel is to have world recognition for Jerusalem as its capital, it will have to let part of the city become the Palestinian capital.

In averring that Indyk's absence from the celebrations should awaken Israelis to the gravity of the challenge, Beilin has performed a service. Israel must realize that the time for fateful choices is near. The government will have to decide whether to fight for Rabin's vision of "an undivided Jerusalem, Israel's capital forever," or satisfy the expectations of the world community and relinquish half the city to a Palestinian police state. And as the American shunning of the celebrations should make clear, if it chooses the former route, it will have to go it alone.

Verbal Violence
October 12, 1995

When President Ezer Weizman speaks, he has not only the moral force of his office behind him, but the personal credibility he has acquired in a lifetime of straightforwardness. And when he inveighs, as he did yesterday, against "verbal and physical attacks against the prime minister and other ministers," it is easy to agree with him. Verbal violence, yelling "traitor" and "murderer" at leaders of the government, is ugly, despicable, and revolting regardless of the source. And physical assault on leaders is utterly unacceptable and should be severely punished.

But it is precisely because his words carry so much weight that Weizman must be careful not to be swept by fashionable generalizations and misleading news reports. What prompted him to say yesterday that, "This is a blot on Israeli democracy," and "There are forces in Israel that can put an end to such attacks and should do so," was the rowdy behavior of anti-Rabin demonstrators at The Event, the Anglo-Saxon gathering at the Wingate Institute.

Indeed, the few hundred jeering demonstrators were rowdy, uncivil, and an embarrassment to the organizers. Not that they had no right to protest. The circumstances may have been apolitical, but the times are so political that no venue can be off-limits to protesters. Yet venting rage at government policies for a few minutes is one thing; making it virtually impossible for the elected prime minister of Israel to be heard is quite another.

The shameful incident recalled the unconscionable yelling that prevented Weizman from speaking to the crowd gathered at the site of the Jerusalem bus bombing in August, or the jeering by Vietnam protesters which made it impossible for then-U.S. president Lyndon Johnson to speak in public in the last months of his tenure.

But it must be noted that not one shout of "traitor," "murderer," or any other violent epithets could be heard. The yelling was confined to legitimate heckling - "Go home," "Resign," "The people have not signed" - and just plain booing.

Nor was there any attempt to attack Prime Minister Yitzhak Rabin physically. The one man who rushed towards Rabin as he entered the grounds was played up in all the media, but he did not seem violent. He was carried off by one of the bodyguards and was not detained.

Speaking to reporters, Rabin called the demonstrators "Kahanists [extreme right-wing followers of Kahana], racists, and a blot on the Jewish people." That he was furious with the crowd was neither surprising nor unjustified. But it is plainly untrue that those who so lustily yelled against him were racist hooligans. Unlike the Kach activists who exploit street demonstrations to display their capacity for scurrility, exhibitionism, and violence, the Wingate protesters were mostly family men and women with children, from all English-speaking countries, who said they were protesting not only Rabin's policies, but his own invective.

Some specifically cited the tongue-lashing Rabin administered to American Jews on his recent Washington visit. Others pointed to what they considered the greatest insult they had endured by the government: "being told to go back where we came from." This ultimate verbal slap, traditionally used by bigots against immigrants in America, was once flung not by Rabin, but "by his Foreign Minister Shimon Peres," as one protester put it, against a woman immigrant from the U.S. who happens to be a Holocaust survivor.

Clearly, the unprecedented invective used against American Jews in the U.S. and Israelis from English-speaking countries, particularly those living beyond the Green Line [the imaginary border between the West Bank and the rest of Israel], has hit home much more effectively than expected. And neither Rabin nor Peres seem to realize that even moderate elements in the Anglo-Saxon community feel offended by it.

Nor do Rabin and his ministers seem particularly disturbed by the reaction to this invective. According to Industry and Trade Minister Micha Harish, they actually welcome it. "The Likud is to blame for extreme right-wing outbursts against Prime Minister Yitzhak Rabin and the Likud will pay a heavy electoral price for this," he maintained yesterday. And as if to prove that he can escalate the invective with the best of them, he added, "We are facing fascism."

Labor clearly hopes, not unreasonably, that unruly, boorish protest, particularly if it deteriorates into real violence, will produce a backlash against the whole opposition, most specifically the Likud's candidate for the premiership, Binyamin Netanyahu.

It is something the protesters at Wingate who made Rabin appear like a righteous victim of a jeering mob should contemplate. But mostly it is Weizman who should realize that the issue transcends the problem of hooliganism. Uncontrolled tensions between rival camps, exacerbated by irresponsible pronouncements by leaders, can only harm national cohesion and unity. It is Weizman's duty as president to condemn the folly of all forms of verbal violence, whether emanating from below or above. Unless the language of the debate in this election year comes under control soon, the consequences to the national fabric will be dire indeed.

U.S. Recognition of Jerusalem
October 15, 1995

For the first time since the seat of government was moved to Jerusalem in 1950, American recognition of Jerusalem as Israel's capital seems likely. Such recognition has been promised by candidates for the U.S. presidency for over 20 years. But "the permanent government" - the State Department bureaucracy - has always managed to annul these promises by warning that the U.S. would lose its status as "honest broker" if they were fulfilled. As a result, the only country in the world in whose capital the U.S. does not maintain an embassy is Israel, America's democratic friend and strategic ally.

Now, with a bill initiated by Republican Senator Jon Kyl of Arizona and co-sponsored by senators Bob Dole (R.-Kansas), Daniel Patrick Moynihan (D.-New York) and Daniel Inouye (D.-Hawaii), Washington may be on the way to moving the American Embassy to Jerusalem.

The first step in this direction was taken earlier this year by Kyl, who - in consultation with former deputy assistant secretary of defense Douglas Feith - formulated a bill which linked Congressional appropriations for the State Department's "Acquisition and Maintenance of Buildings Abroad" fund to groundbreaking for the embassy in Jerusalem in 1996. Co-sponsored by Senate Majority leader Dole, who is also the front-running Republican presidential candidate, the bill garnered the support of 62 senators. But Secretary of State Warren Christopher threatened to recommend a presidential veto, which seemed to inhibit further support for the bill.

The official reason for the possible veto was that linking a threat to withhold funds with requiring the administration to act was unconstitutional. (Subsequently, experts have ruled that it is not.) The real reason is the traditional fear that Washington would lose its neutral status if it moved its embassy to Jerusalem.

The administration was also encouraged in its opposition to the bill by Israel's lack of enthusiasm for it. While officially supportive of a move which Israel has passionately advocated since David Ben-Gurion's days, government representatives quietly suggested it might harm the peace process. To its credit, the American Jewish lobby AIPAC ignored this trepidation and lobbied for the bill.

The bill introduced on Friday in the Senate (an identical bill is expected in the House of Representatives within days) is not as forceful as the original Kyl proposal. The withholding of funds from the State Department pending groundbreaking for the new embassy in 1996 has been deleted, while allocations for the embassy building (amounting to $100 million) have been made discretionary rather than mandatory. The modifications were introduced to gain greater support, and as a result, Moynihan, one of the administration's mainstays in the Senate, has agreed to join the bill's sponsorship.

But despite the modifications, the bill does mandate the relocation of the American Embassy by May 31, 1999. And, as Kyl put it in a press release on Friday, "If the administration intends to build a new facility for the embassy [by 1999], it will have to break ground in 1996 anyway." Moreover, the new bill not only mandates the embassy's relocation, it has "teeth" in the form of a warning that half the allocation for the State Department building fund in 1999 will not be made unless the administration reports to Congress "that the U.S. Embassy in Jerusalem has officially opened."

The faint-hearted and appeasers in Israel and the U.S. who oppose the bill because it may irritate the PLO should heed Kyl's Friday statement: "The status of Jerusalem is not, never was, and never will be negotiable. . . . The United States is not neutral about Jewish rights in the ancient Jewish homeland or in Jerusalem. I believe the key to our diplomatic effectiveness is not our neutrality, but our power and loyalty to our friends and our principles."

Observers in Jerusalem
October 23, 1995

Speaking at the Knesset debate on the Oslo 2 agreement three weeks ago, Foreign Minister Shimon Peres defended the government's decision to let Jerusalem Arabs vote in the elections for the Palestinian Council. Dismissing opposition claims that council elections impinge on Israeli sovereignty in the city, he said Arab voting affects Israel's rights no more than voting in U.S. elections by American residents of Paris affects the sovereignty of the French capital.

Leaving aside the most obvious difference between the two situations - that American expatriates do not claim Paris as their capital - there is a fundamental contradiction between this Oslo 2 provision and the government's repeated vows that Jerusalem will forever stay the undivided capital of Israel.

As Mayor Ehud Olmert pointed out in an interview published yesterday in *Ha'aretz*, the government is perpetrating "a fraud and a swindle" on the people of Israel. "There is an intolerable gap between the government's pronouncements on its professed allegiance to an undivided Jerusalem, the capital of Israel forever and ever under Israel sovereignty, and its actions and inactions on the ground . . . the cynicism is horrendous."

The actions and inactions to which Olmert refers are worrisome indeed. The government has done nothing about the hundreds of armed Palestinian plainclothesmen, members of Jibril Rajoub's Preventive Security force in Jericho, who are operating as law enforcers among Jerusalem Arabs. Nor has it closed the unofficial courts established by the PA, which resolve disputes among Jerusalem Arabs, or the PA's government offices - including the PA's foreign ministry at Orient House - still operating openly and freely in the city.

But nothing can undermine Israel's authority more dramatically than the coming elections. That Jerusalem Arabs can conduct a separate census, vote in the PA elections, and be elected to the Palestinian Council would have been tolerable had they all voters been declared foreign citizens casting absentee ballots by mail. But the city's Arab residents will be able to campaign in the city, hold election rallies, and vote in several designated polling places.

Defending the procedure in a talk with American Jewish leaders on Friday, Prime Minister Yitzhak Rabin said that the Arab voters will have to mail their ballots "in envelopes carrying Israeli stamps." But this is simply not so.

According to the sixth clause of the Oslo 2 election protocol, Arab voters will receive a registration card from the Palestinian Central Election Committee, in which their polling place will be designated. On election day, they will identify themselves to the committee representative at the polling place and receive voting slips, one for the council and one for its president. They will then deposit their ballots in containers (carefully not named ballot boxes, but to all intents and purposes precisely that), which will be transported at the end of the day to the regional election depot.

The polling places will be in five post offices, but the ballots will not be mailed, nor will any other postal services be used. In fact, there will be no difference whatsoever between the voting in Jerusalem and elsewhere in the Palestinian areas.

By far the most ominous part of this arrangement is that international inspectors will be allowed to supervise the elections in Jerusalem as well as in the territories. This, more than anything else, is a direct challenge to Israel's sovereignty. As Olmert aptly put it, "UN observers in Jerusalem belong to a bygone era. Whoever returns UN inspectors to Jerusalem turns Israel back to the 1950s. . . . It is an admission that the eastern part of the city is not under our absolute sovereignty." To carry Peres's analogy to its conclusion, one must wonder if the French government would allow UN observers to supervise Americans voting in Paris.

Not surprisingly, Olmert's suspicions about the government's intentions are magnified by its indifference to the revelations about PA money used for illegal activities in Jerusalem in letters displayed by MK Ze'ev Begin (Likud) on television. Even more worrisome is that the original Oslo architects are now developing a "compromise" on Jerusalem.

Ron Pundak and Ya'ir Hirshfeld, who initiated the process under the guidance of then-deputy foreign minister Yossi Beilin, are working in collaboration with Faisal Husseini's staff on a plan which, Olmert says, will inevitably lead to the division of sovereignty in Jerusalem. Concomitantly, Orient House officials have been leaking to the press that the PLO is no longer insisting on exclusive rule over all the areas Israel won in 1967. In some of the suburbs and the Old City's Jewish quarter, they say, the Palestinians are willing to share control. ("Sharing" a city is probably impossible even between democracies. Between a police state and a democracy it is utterly unthinkable.)

Olmert is concerned about the effect of these developments on Israelis. Misleading the public about Jerusalem may generate uncontrollable protests, he fears. "This is not Jericho. This is not a bypass. This is heartbreak road," he said. But even more dangerous is that the expectations of the city's Arab population are being raised to a pitch which will make any arrangement short of redividing the city into two sovereignties an invitation to endless strife and violence.

Jerusalem: Good and Bad News
October 25, 1995

The good news is that a bill stating that the U.S. recognizes Jerusalem as the capital of Israel was yesterday passed in the Senate by an overwhelming majority of 93 to 5. The bill was expected to pass by a similarly crushing majority in the House of Representatives last night, and be signed into law by President Bill Clinton in the coming weeks despite the White House's pro forma objection to the bill.

The bill's language is unequivocal. Under the headline "Statement of the policy of the United States" it says: "Jerusalem should remain an undivided city in which the rights of every ethnic and religious group are protected; Jerusalem should be recognized as the capital of the state of Israel; and the United States Embassy in Israel should be established in Jerusalem no later than May 31, 1999."

And it has some teeth, too. It withholds 50 percent of the State Department's funding for maintaining embassies in fiscal year 1999 unless the U.S. declares that the Jerusalem embassy has opened.

The bad news is that the original bill, proposed by Senator Jon Kyl of Arizona and sponsored by leading Republicans and Democrats, has been watered down to accommodate the administration and the Israeli government, both fearful of its impact on the negotiations with the PLO.

According to the compromise version, the president will be able to suspend the move of the American embassy to Jerusalem at six month intervals "to protect the national security interests of the United States." There is no limit to the number of times the president can exercise this privilege.

Senator Robert Dole of Kansas, the bill's main sponsor and the leading Republican contender for the presidency, has inserted a "colloquy" with Kyl in the Congressional Record, which asserts the presidential waiver is strictly limited. It is meant to be "interpreted narrowly," Dole stressed, so that the president cannot "infinitely" delay the embassy's opening.

But the fact is that if Clinton or his successor feel that the embassy's move should not occur until the "final status" talks with the PLO are concluded, the "Jerusalem Embassy Act of 1995" will be vitiated. Only the physical move of the embassy offices and the ambassador's residence to the capital will make world recognition of Israel's capital a fact of life.

The bill's passage was intended to greet Prime Minister Yitzhak Rabin on his visit to Washington today, as a gesture on the occasion of Jerusalem's 3,000th anniversary. But it also emphasizes some intrinsic weaknesses in Israel's position. Israel is the only country whose capital the U.S. and most of the world's governments do not recognize as such, and it is the only country whose government feels it must tacitly undermine efforts to have its capital recognized for fear that it might antagonize its adversaries.

An even sadder commentary on Israel's position on Jerusalem is a recent declaration by the Oslo agreement's chief architect, Minister for Economic Planning Yossi Beilin. Published a day before virtually the whole U.S. Congress voted that Jerusalem must remain undivided, Beilin's pronouncement favors dividing the city between Israeli and Palestinian sovereignties. That Rabin called Beilin's proposal irresponsible is hardly comforting. As one prominent commentator has out it, what Beilin declares today, Foreign Minister Shimon Peres adopts tomorrow, and Rabin signs the day after.

A Black Day for the Whole Jewish Nation
November 5, 1995

The shock is universal. No Israeli, no Jew, no decent human being anywhere can help being shaken to the core, shattered to the depth of his and her soul by the news of the assassination of Prime Minister Yitzhak Rabin.

Nothing, absolutely nothing, is a greater blow to the life of the Jewish nation than fraternal violence, and nothing makes such violence more threatening to the nation's future than the assassination of the head of government.

No nation has suffered more from what is known in Hebrew as "fraternal hatred" or "hatred without cause." In Jewish tradition, such hatred is blamed for the destruction of the Second Temple. Had such hatred not splintered the nation at crucial junctures of its existence, the history of the Jewish people would have been different.

If the Jewish nation is again unlucky, Rabin's death last night from an assassin's bullet may well be remembered as a blow from which Israel has not recovered.

But if the nation is more fortunate than in the past and reason prevails, the assassination will serve as a reminder that internal violence is the most dangerous enemy, most incurable scourge, and most irredeemable national disaster.

It would be neither realistic nor relevant to ask for national unity on political issues at this point. But all decent men and women in this country must unite in making violence by Jews against Jews utterly and eternally unacceptable. Nothing less than the nation's fate depends on it.

World Statesman
November 6, 1995

If the opinions of scores of diverse nations count, then Yitzhak Rabin has already been given the accolade of greatness. Expressions of regret and outrage are to be expected when the leader of a democracy is gunned down, but the outpouring of shock and grief from the nations of the world over his assassination has been truly astounding.

Of course the leaders of the United States, the European Union, Russia, and the large Asian states would be expected to pay tribute to one of their colleagues - nothing less is expected in civilized international relations. But the most amazing outburst of international rage was to be found on the new modern forum of the ordinary person - the global computer Internet. Several bulletin boards were utterly swamped by grief-stricken sympathizers and the biggest Internet provider, the U.S.-based CompuServe, was forced to open a special forum for condolences, when its popular Israel Forum became overloaded.

If those who dubbed Rabin "a traitor" have always been a tiny minority in Israel, then it is clear that in the international community such sentiments are non-existent.

Whatever controversies Rabin's polices raised in Israel, it is clear that foreign observers have gone to the heart of the matter and see him in the same light as the late Anwar Sadat -

a man who made war when he felt he had to, and then risked all to become a maker of peace. As with Sadat, it was this courageous change that led him to this rendezvous with death.

Whatever the final outcome of the peace process, the world has universally anointed Rabin as the architect of Israel's new relationship not only with the Arabs, but with the community of nations.

"I knew Yitzhak Rabin well," said President Jacques Chirac of France, whose words typify the sentiments pouring out of almost every country. "I knew the man of combat, who contributed so much to give Israel its security. I knew the man of peace, the visionary statesman who, with courage and lucidity, chose dialogue and reconciliation between the peoples of the region. And then I knew the man himself, a man of conviction but also a man of passion, a man of the heart."

It is easy to forget how recently Israel felt isolated and alone in the Cold War world community, with few warm friends in a sea of hostility. Now to see condolences and expressions of sympathy pouring into Israel from India, China, Russia, Ukraine, Slovakia, and South America is a reminder of how far we have come in such a short time.

An Irish patriot being executed in the fight for independence said from the dock: "When my country takes its place among the nations of the earth, then, and not till then, let my epitaph be written." Yitzhak Rabin's epitaph can be written now.

Assassination as National Trauma
The London Daily Telegraph
November 6, 1995

Nothing in the lexicon of contemporary politics can explain what the assassination of Prime Minister Yitzhak Rabin's means to Israelis. Comparisons with other political murders, like the Kennedy or Sadat assassinations, are inapplicable. The impact of Rabin's assassination can only be understood by remembering that the Jews are the only people still experiencing a national trauma which occurred almost 2,000 years ago. The destruction of Jerusalem and the Second Temple in the year 70 A.D. is not only mentioned in daily prayers and commemorated on an annual fasting day. It is studied by every schoolchild as a morality tale, as the supreme historic tragedy of national misdirection. And the cause of this tragedy, according to Jewish tradition, was not Roman might or Judean frailty. The destruction of the Temple and the exile that followed were the result of fraternal hatred, the "hatred without cause" so passionately condemned by Jewish sages, which brought on civil strife, internecine killing and finally bitter defeat.

Whether this tradition is historically sound is irrelevant. What matters is that the manifestation of internal violence, the violence of Jew against Jew, rekindles the ancient trauma in the Jewish collective memory with explosive force. Deemed far more dangerous than an external enemy, it is viewed as an incurable scourge, an irredeemable national disaster. And it is the specter of precisely this kind of disaster which Israel sees in the killing of Rabin.

On the face of it, Rabin's murderer Yigal Amir was no more than an unhinged young man, an otherwise "normal" student who suddenly heard God telling him to kill the Prime Minister. He belonged to a tiny fringe organization known for extremist views, advocacy of violence and — mostly — for bragging about crimes it never committed. Most recently, it took responsibility for the killing of an Arab villager near Hebron, but the man was found to have been murdered by local Arab criminals.

According to the police, this extremist group had nothing to do with the assassination. Amir acted alone. He had attempted to kill Rabin twice before, but could not break through his bodyguards. This time he saw an opening and used it. Evil at its most capricious and banal, it would seem.

Yet Amir is not just a man who hears voices. He is also an ideologue. Unlike the would-be assassin who in 1957 tried to kill Israel's first Prime Minister David Ben Gurion to avenge a personal gripe against a government agency, he cannot be dismissed as just a mental case. His hatred for Rabin is a function of his feeling of betrayal by the government. Not a personal betrayal, but what he perceives as a "sell out" of the nation for the sake of a fake, deadly peace. For Amir, Rabin was not just an appeaser, a Neville Chamberlain, but a Marshall Henri Petain, an erstwhile war hero who collaborates with the nation's mortal enemy.

In viewing Rabin and the government as traitorous, Amir is not alone. And while he may be the only one in the country who would translate such a belief to murder, he represents — albeit in an unacceptable, violent version — the alienation and the sense of betrayal felt by a large part of the population. In fact, not since the state's infancy has Israel suffered from such polarization between government and opposition.

The dichotomy is caused not by differences over peace as a goal. Everyone in Israel wants peace and no one believes war can solve the Arab-Israeli conflict. The differences are over the wisdom of the Oslo agreements: whether they can bring peace, as the government and most of the world believe, or precipitate war, as Israel's opposition parties, representing a majority of the country's Jewish population, are convinced they will. The two sides have drastically different perceptions of the changes in the Arab world. The governing coalition views these changes as momentous transformations, similar to the collapse of the Soviet empire. The opposition are convinced the changes are tactical, and at best confined to the ruling classes. The abiding popular hatred for Israel in the Arab world, the desire to destroy the Jewish state, is still a primary Arab goal, they feel.

In Israel these are questions of life and death. Those who oppose the Oslo agreements truly fear that giving up strategic areas will endanger the very existence of the country. Others are certain that in the absence of a peace agreement now, the country will be embroiled in a devastating war. The 'anti's see in Oslo the end of the Zionist dream. The 'pro's view the agreements as the first step to a thriving, peaceful and prosperous Middle East in which Israel will play a major role.

Under the circumstances, it is hardly surprising that the invective on both sides has been harsh and uncivilized. The vulgarities and scurrilities of opposition demonstrators have received all the publicity. Signs calling Rabin and members of his government traitors and murderers have been shown on world television. One incident, in which a picture of Rabin in Gestapo uniform was carried by a demonstrator who belonged to the late Rabbi Kahana's movement Kach [an extreme right-wing party], was particularly revolting.

But it must be said that the government is not guiltless in this escalation of vehemence. Rabin himself contributed to the acrimonious tone by using the kind of invective against his opponents which no prime minister in the democratic world would use today. The opposition, he said, were the natural allies of the murderous Islamic Hamas organization. The settlers were nothing but a burden, parasites, a cancer in the nation's body. He even heaped calumny and contempt on

Golan residents, members of his own Labor party, who protested his intention to evacuate the Golan as the price of a peace agreement with Syria.

This insensitivity to the very real anguish and anxiety felt by residents of the territories, all of whom were there at the behest and encouragement of Israeli governments, only exacerbated tensions. That the government had only the slimmest of majorities for policies which would affect the fate of the nation for generations did little to ameliorate these tensions, particularly since the majority in the Knesset relied on the votes of the anti-Zionist Arab parties. Even President Weizman, a certified dove who initially enthusiastically supported the Oslo agreements, expressed grave misgivings about the government's seeming rush to make concessions despite Yasser Arafat's failure to live up to his commitments.

Yet despite the tensions, there seemed to be little concern about violence against public officials. Rabin himself adamantly refused to hear of wearing a bullet-proof vest. And he angrily rejected suggestions by his party that he be accompanied by "volunteers" who would forcibly remove demonstrators from his path.

But now all this has changed. The talk of the slippery slope to a civil war is no longer dismissed as the nightmare of terminal pessimists. As the moment of truth approaches, as the decision on the removal of settlements becomes more imminent, as more Arab towns are evacuated and left to the uncertain vigilance of the Palestinian police, the opponents of the Oslo agreement feel more desperate. There are various dreaded scenarios. Ordered to abandon their towns and villages, the settlers may resist the army with firearms; or a minor incident involving the Palestinian police will flare up into a shooting match which the army will be assigned to resolve, leading to a firefight with the settlers; or another assassination will launch a series of political murders. The possibilities seem as realistic as they are numerous.

Yet it may well be that the assassination will act as a sobering shock. It is, after all, an unprecedented act in Israel's history. At first, the blame will fall on the opposition, which will inevitably be on the defensive. But both sides may step more carefully through the minefields of the bitter debate. Reason may prevail, issues discussed with civility, differences settled strictly at the ballot box.

And what of the peace process? As is often the case, political assassins achieve the opposite of what they aim for. The revulsion against their deed is transformed into a concerted effort to fulfill the wishes of the victim, the martyr to the cause. It may well be that in his death Rabin will have achieved the consensus in support of the peace agreements which he could not achieve in his life.

Much now depends on what the Arab side will do. If the shock of the killing gives the Palestinians pause, if they realize that terror can spin matters out of control, and that violence, once stirred, may harm them at least as much as it would harm Israel, they may shun terrorism. If, on the other hand, they view the assassination as a sign of Israeli disunity and weakness, they may be tempted to pounce in for the kill with more violence.

For the next year, the Prime Minister will be Shimon Peres. For all his penchant for Pollyannish views, he is a consummate diplomat whose skills are second to none. If he realizes that soothing the worries of Israelis is as important as accommodating the wishes of the Palestinians, he may have a much-needed healing influence. It would be neither realistic nor relevant to expect national unity on political issues at this point. But Israel is so hungry for a soothing word from its leaders that it should not take a superhuman effort to turn an unprecedented tragedy into the beginning of national recovery.

Wanted: A Healing
November 7, 1995

Israel is not a superpower whose favors and protection are sought by the nations of the world, but not since John F. Kennedy's funeral in 1963 has there been an assembly of world leaders like yesterday's gathering in Jerusalem in tribute to Yitzhak Rabin. It was almost as if Zion had really become a light unto the nations, as if the love of peace had replaced the awe of power.

It was not, of course, an ordinary funeral of an Israeli premier. Like all events honoring assassinated leaders, it was not just an event of state but a protest by the world establishment against anarchy and murder, a demonstration on behalf of civilization and order.

But the appearance of more than 80 monarchs, presidents and prime ministers on a cemetery hill in Jerusalem - a capital the vast majority of them do not recognize - for the unceremonious burial of a tiny country's premier cannot be perceived as merely an expression of solidarity. Rabin was much more than a colleague slain in the line of duty. He represented - to risk a cliche - the eternal hope for a better world.

If there is one area of the world in which peace seems elusive if not utterly impossible, it is the Middle East. This is true not only because of the century-old conflict between Jews and Arabs over the same piece of land, nor just the fierce Moslem opposition to the existence of "infidel" sovereignties in the region. Much of the strife in the area has nothing to do with Israel's existence. As the Gulf War proved most recently, and as the continuing belligerency of Iran, Iraq, Libya and Syria show now, the area's turmoil is as endemic as it is threatening to world peace.

But by taking steps which previous Israeli governments had deemed unthinkable and reaching an agreement with the

PLO, Rabin inspired hope that even the seemingly insurmountable can be conquered. True, he caused a sharp split in Israel by doing so, but the world community - hopeful that he would neutralize one of the world's most volatile powderkegs - became his fan club.

What has given this trend a special boost was the unstinting support of the U.S. In the absence of any real competition, the U.S., the only true superpower, sets the tone in world politics. Had it ignored Rabin, the rest of the world would have found it difficult to work up much enthusiasm for his initiatives. But President Bill Clinton's devotion and friendship, the tireless mediation efforts of the American diplomatic team headed by Secretary of State Warren Christopher, and the Israeli access to the American corridors of power have all made Israel a global factor quite disproportionate to its size.

It is most likely that Israel will continue to be such a factor in the foreseeable future. If anything, Rabin's death may increase world sympathy for his unfinished plans. Nor are the leaders who paid him tribute yesterday unaware of Acting Prime Minister Shimon Peres's contribution to the process. On the contrary. Most undoubtedly know that the architect and begetter of the Oslo agreements is Peres, and that Rabin - the military hero - provided mostly the necessary credibility for the risks these agreements entail.

It should not, then, be difficult for Peres to continue receiving world support and encouragement. If anything, it may be easier now to get the richer countries to contribute to the Palestinian economy and thus realize his dream of a more prosperous Palestinian entity.

But it would be a mistake for Peres to believe that world support is all he needs to complete the task he and Rabin began. As one Israeli politician has put it, peace with the Palestinians cannot be achieved if there is no peace inside Israel. There are many who view the agreements with the

PLO as blunders which may invite war rather than bring peace. It is their right to have doubts about the government's policies and to oppose them with all legal means.

But the vast majority of these opponents will dutifully follow the national majority's decisions. To try to delegitimize them now through charges that they share the guilt of Rabin's assassination is to inflame internal conflicts to a danger point. Peres's first duty as prime minister must be to relieve tensions, heal the open wounds, and call for reasoned and civilized debate. He is considered one of the world's most skilled diplomats. Let him use these skills in Israel first.

Negotiations Over Jerusalem

December 8, 1995

Rumors that senior Israeli and Palestinian representatives are discussing Jerusalem's future have been circulating for some time now. But only this week has Ziad Abu Zayyad, a PLO leader who chairs the Palestinian delegation on arms control, confirmed these contacts. Abu Zayyad himself seems to be a participant in the discussions on the Palestinian side, while the Israeli team consists of the same academics who began the secret Oslo process in 1992. Close to Yossi Beilin, now minister at the prime minister's office, they almost certainly represent Prime Minister Shimon Peres's views as well.

The Palestinians may be examining the proposals floated by the Beilin team with interest. But they are primarily eager to establish facts on the ground before the official "final status" talks begin in May. What they have achieved so far is quite impressive.

The Peres letter on Jerusalem, whose existence was first denied and then confirmed by the government, granted Israeli consent to the activities of PLO offices in Jerusalem.

These were presumably intended to be strictly non-political, but the Palestinian institutions in the city, particularly Orient House, have become to all intents and purposes the Palestinian Authority's Jerusalem ministries and administrative offices.

Mayor Ehud Olmert has vowed to curb their activities and shut down Orient House, but he has neither the power nor the means to do so, and the government is obviously unwilling to sour relations with the PA by closing them.

An even more concrete achievement has been the agreement to allow the city's Arab residents not only to vote in the elections for the Palestinian Council but to run as candidates for office. And, as if to confirm the tenuousness of Israel's sovereignty in the city, international observers will be allowed to monitor the elections. This is an unmistakable signal that at least in one part of the city Israel's sovereignty is negotiable.

To say that all this is in dramatic conflict with the government's official position on Jerusalem is to understate the case. Earlier this week, on the occasion of the posthumous bestowal of an honorary Jerusalem citizenship on Yitzhak Rabin, Peres reiterated Labor's traditional position. The city must stay undivided under Israeli sovereignty. It cannot accommodate the capitals of two states.

The truth of this statement is self evident. No city has ever been both undivided and "shared," which is what some Palestinian leaders and their "peace camp" supporters in Israel say they want. Even if the two governments were democracies, the complications of such sharing would be enormous. With one state a democracy and the other a police state, it is unthinkable.

The city can, of course, be divided again. Presumably, this is what the Palestinians hope will eventually happen, giving them control of the area of the city that was under Jordanian occupation between 1948 and 1967. But such a solution would be unacceptable to a vast majority of Israelis.

Nor is it clear that the city's Arab residents are eager to live under a PLO regime. Registration for the Palestinian Council elections has been slow, with fewer than half the eligible Arab voters in Jerusalem signing up. Most Jerusalem Arabs are afraid to lose their many privileges as permanent residents of Israel.

Moreover, in the past few months thousands of Arab residents have lined up in Interior Ministry offices to apply for Israeli citizenship. They obviously hope that as Israelis, they will be able to move out of the eastern part of Jerusalem if the final settlement lets the PLO assume control there.

It has been a given since the establishment of Israel that Jerusalem is one of the toughest problems in the Arab-Israeli conflict, which is why it has been left to the last stages of the talks. With the moment of truth approaching, it is difficult to discern a solution acceptable to both sides.

Reportedly, the Israeli team is suggesting expanding Jerusalem's borders to include some of the neighboring villages and towns, thus enabling Israel to withdraw from them without actually dividing the city. But it is doubtful that the Palestinian Authority will be satisfied with a capital based in Azariya or Ramallah.

Yasser Arafat repeatedly vows to continue the jihad until the Palestinian flag is hoisted over the churches and mosques of Jerusalem and the city becomes the Palestinian capital. And Abu Zayyad has said, "If we fail to reach a solution on Jerusalem, we will be heading for a religious war over the city. I don't think the people would be enthusiastic over a jihad."

It is this not-so-veiled threat which the Palestinians assume will win the day. They believe that faced with the choice between a peace agreement with a divided Jerusalem and a jihad, Israel will discard brave slogans about Israel's undivided capital and opt for the former.

It will not be long before their assumption will be tested.

Security in Jerusalem
December 20, 1995

Maj-Gen. Ilan Biran has denied that in a Sunday meeting with Jerusalem municipal officials he expressed pessimism about security in the city after the army evacuates neighboring Ramallah and Bethlehem. On the contrary, he said the following day. He feels the security services have the situation well in hand, adding that he had meant to reassure his audience rather than cause concern.

Yet it is difficult to be sanguine about the latest developments in the capital. Jerusalem police chief Arye Amit has prepared a list of 70 entryways through which Palestinian residents of the territories enter Jerusalem without permits and subject to no Israeli control. Since there is no intention to build a fence around the city or to block these entrances, Jerusalemites must assume that this massive daily migration will continue unfettered.

Residents of Jerusalem's southern and northern sections have received instructions on precautions they should take now that the neighboring towns will be under Palestinian Authority control. The instructions contain warnings to increase alertness, install alarm systems and protect homes with grilles and dogs. At one spot, the army has erected an electronic barrier, but every morning cars from neighboring Arab villages easily circumvent it on their way to Jerusalem.

Even more worrisome is an internal security document which reveals that the Palestinian Authority has been organizing youth units on the pattern of the organizations active during the intifada. Their members are being prepared to mount attacks on Israelis once the "final status" talks are launched in May and the next phase in the struggle for the eastern part of the city begins.

Jerusalem is not like other urban areas suddenly turned into border towns by Oslo 2. Not only is the city an immediate, prime target of the PLO and an essential component of its demands for a Palestinian state with Jerusalem as its capital. It is a mixed city almost a third of whose population is Arab. With Israel's acquiescence, it is also a center of PA government office buildings, treated by the government as extra-territorial domains.

Only lately has the government shown some signs of concern about the PA's creeping encroachment. Several PA conferences, for example, have been canceled by the police. But once elections to the Palestinian Council are held in the eastern part of the city, and international recognition of the Council's legitimacy is granted, the efforts to keep Jerusalem Israel's undivided capital will assume a new dimension. It will be then that Biran's security assurances will be truly tested.

Shahal and Internal Security
December 28, 1995

Hearing Minister of Internal Security Moshe Shahal's comments on the country's internal security problems leaves one wondering if he is the minister in charge or a visitor from parts unknown.

On Sunday, he warned that the Russian mafia is about to take over Israel by acquiring companies, properties, and politicians. Coming from the minister, this is quite a puzzling accusation. If foreign criminals are buying into Israeli businesses, it would be nice to know which ones are affected. If these same criminals are breaking the laws of the land, it would be interesting to hear what the police are doing about it. And it would be particularly comforting to know that the Internal Security Ministry has an updated list of their names. Otherwise, uncharitable souls may believe that crying "mafia" is no more than an easy way to capture headlines.

Most curious is the charge that the mafia is trying to gain control of politicians here, "just as has happened in the rest of the world." One can only assume that Shahal is expecting a major scandal to break any minute, something on the scale of the Italian government scandal. It would be nice to know who the corrupt politicians are, and what exactly they do for their mafia bosses. Otherwise, suspicious observers may believe the whole story is a pre-primaries canard.

Shahal is also deeply concerned about the flood of car thefts. With 100 vehicles stolen every day, Israel is the world leader in this field. Most of the stolen cars are transported to the self-rule areas, never to be seen again. And since these areas are only hundreds of meters away, the thieves are having an easy time of it.

To his credit, Shahal has made no bones about his position on this issue. He is definitely opposed to car thefts, and with commendable courage he expresses his unqualified objections freely and openly on radio talk shows and press conferences. But he has yet to come up with a solitary idea on how to fight the plague. Unless, that is, he considers it an irresistible force majeure, a phenomenon against which plain mortals are helpless.

Shahal also definitely opposes the spread of drugs. With the conscientiousness one expects only from the best of citizens, he warns of their destructive effect on the nation's youth. Yet some taxpayers wonder if they may expect something more from the nation's No. 1 law enforcer. Some even want the august ministry to do something about other scourges, like traffic accidents. It is, after all, Shahal's ministerial responsibility to apprehend violators of traffic laws. Yet the much vaunted introduction of traffic policemen to the highways seems to be the country's best kept secret.

Serious as they may be, these cavils pale against Shahal's Knesset statement on Tuesday. In what must be the most extraordinary admission made by a police minister in Israel's history, he said he had not known until the preceding day that only the Border Police operates in the eastern part of Jerusalem. It is as if that half of the city were a border settlement, he said.

It is now more than three years since Shahal became minister of police (now minister of internal security). Yet he did not know that the blue-uniformed police do not move in half of the capital. For at least 18 months of this period, the media have been running stories about the complete freedom with which a foreign police force — not the Russian mafia but Jibril Rajoub's Preventive Security Police based in Jericho — has been running its own "law enforcement" and protection racket in Jerusalem. Its operatives have been kidnapping Arab residents with impunity and dragging them to the Jericho prison, where they are tortured and sometimes killed.

There is even a judicial network run by city Arabs, to which not only its Arab residents, but Jews who have disputes with Arabs, often resort, bypassing the Israeli courts.

Shahal need not go far to find an example of PLO forces usurping the authority of his police force. For Christmas Day, Yasser Arafat ordered the Arab papers to feature on their front pages a photograph of himself embracing the Greek Orthodox Patriarch Deodoros. The accompanying story reported that the patriarch had declared himself the spiritual heir to Sofronius — who in 638 handed the keys of the Church of the Holy Sepulchre to the Moslem Caliph Omar Ibn al-Khattab — and welcomed Arafat as Omar's heir. (It may be useful to note that when Omar's forces occupied Jerusalem, the Jews were not allowed to stay.)

One journalist, *Al Quds* editor Maher Alameh, failed to follow Arafat's orders. He was promptly ordered to report to Rajoub's headquarters in Jericho, and when he refused, he was forcibly kidnapped from his Jerusalem home by Rajoub's secret police, 400 of whom are freely operating in the city. As of last night, Alameh — a man who undoubtedly thought he had Shahal's protection — was still in the Jericho jail. This time Shahal has not even made it known whether he opposes kidnappings, in what is daily referred to by the government as Israel's eternal capital.

On Tuesday, Shahal announced in the Knesset that 500 men have been added to the police force to guard the holy places in Jerusalem. Considering his performance to date, it must be hoped that none of these sites ends up in Jericho.

The Election Festival
January 21, 1996

There was probably an element of truth in what former U.S. president Jimmy Carter said yesterday in Jerusalem — the Palestinian election may indeed signal a new beginning for Palestinians and for the whole region. But if Carter meant that this new dawn will be characterized by the flowering of democracy and the ubiquitous observance of human rights he is as wrong as he proved to be so often in the past. It is far more likely that what Israel and the world witnessed yesterday was the birth of the 23rd Arab police state.

It was almost 20 years ago, soon after he became president, that Carter inveighed against "the inordinate fear of Communism" and chastised those who considered Leonid Brezhnev anything less than benign. It took the Soviet invasion of Afghanistan — a direct result of his policies of appeasement — to "open his eyes," as he put it. This eye-opening cost millions their lives and homes, but it did not wean Carter of his sympathy for autocrats, among whom Yasser Arafat has always had a special spot.

There can be little doubt about the autocratic nature of yesterday's election. It was no different from elections in the old Soviet Union or in today's Egypt. Demonstrating a touch of sophistication which other Arab despots lack, Arafat encouraged an obscure 72-year-old woman to run against him for the Palestinian presidency, while suppressing any challenge by opponents with a real following.

Similarly, he took no chances with candidates for the Palestinian Council. Yesterday's voters had a choice between candidates who were vigorously endorsed by Arafat and those he merely approved. Even if a few of the self-styled "independents" get elected, they are most likely to follow the Egyptian pattern, where out of the 114 independents elected to the 444-seat parliament, a full 1000 suddenly saw the light immediately after the election and joined the ruling National Democratic Party.

Carter is hardly unique in his beaming approval of yesterday's exercise. The 700 international election observers (including, perhaps appropriately, some from such bastions of democracy as Egypt and Yemen) will give the election a stamp of legitimacy. Even the observers who spent some time in the country before the balloting and who witnessed the Palestinian Authority's pre-campaign manipulation and suppression of the media, the arrest, intimidation and bribery of unwanted candidates and their staff, and the hate-filled campaign rhetoric calling for Israel's destruction will undoubtedly not allow facts to get in the way of the fairy tale the world wants to hear.

Unfortunately, the government is fully supportive of this farce. It is no secret that it has done everything within its power to help its "peace partner" in the election, and it will undoubtedly see in the large turnout a Palestinian vote of confidence in the Oslo agreements and an approval of its policies.

But while it is probably true that the Palestinians approve of the way Arafat has managed to attain Israeli withdrawal from the territories, the fact remains that — as yesterday's election made amply clear — the Palestinian state will be no different from other Arab regimes. Some Israelis may consider an autocratic regime preferable to a democracy. It is, after all, easier to settle matters quickly and efficiently with a dictator than to worry about real parliaments and press.

But theirs is a woefully short-sighted approach. The nascent Palestinian police state being legitimized by yesterday's election is not across a desert nor across a river; it is literally across the street. Like all police states it will be aggression-prone, and in this case it will also be irredentist and revanchist.

This is the first time in history that a democracy has willingly helped establish such a state on the outskirts of its major population centers. One can only hope that the experiment will not be remembered as an example of national self-immolation.

Frauds and Advocates
January 24, 1996

When an Arab journalist told former president Jimmy Carter that the Palestinian elections were so fraud-ridden they could not be taken seriously, Carter said, "If you really want to see election fraud, let me take you to Chicago."

If nothing else, the remark confirms Carter's addiction to "moral equivalence" — the insidious tendency of apologists for tyrants to equate misdemeanors in democracies with murderous enormities in dictatorships.

It is hardly a secret that occasional frauds are committed in some U.S. election districts. But elections there in general are held in an atmosphere of complete freedom and fairness. Every seat is contested, the media are unfettered, freedom of speech is total, all candidates can campaign, complaints of irregularities are thoroughly investigated, and recounts ordered.

In the Palestinian elections voting irregularities were only part of the problem. The disappearance of ballot boxes, multiple voting, vote-counting forgeries, and intimidation and detention of complainants were but a continuation of a pattern established before polling day. In the weeks before January 20, candidates who had won primaries were rubbed off the list by Yasser Arafat, the press was intimidated by kidnappings and arrests, undesirable candidates were threatened or bribed, and Arafat himself ran for the position of "president" without credible opposition.

It should have come, then, as no surprise that after the election in Hebron 40 ballot boxes suddenly disappeared; or that in Gaza candidates who were declared winners after the first count suddenly lost their majority after the second; or, conversely, that declared losers, like Arafat's lieutenant Marwan Kanafani, suddenly became winners; or that in Jerusalem Hanan Ashrawi's initial big majority, which placed her first, suddenly shrank to put her in second place; or that only three women (including Ashrawi) were elected instead of the seven expected to win seats; or that three days after the elections the final results were still unknown.

Perhaps the most typical complaint came from a candidate who lost in Khan Yunis. She admitted that one of her agents had managed to insert 50 fictitious ballots on her behalf, yet she lost because others, she said, cheated more. She obviously had a point. In some districts the number of counted ballots was larger than that of registered voters.

If there is one thing that can be said in favor of the Palestinian elections it is that they were a more sophisticated hoax than, say, elections in Egypt. Hosni Mubarak runs with no competition. Arafat knew that by encouraging a nonentity to run against him, he would look like a truly democratic candidate in the West.

Such elections are hardly unusual in the Middle East. Nor is it surprising that Israel, the E.U. and the U.S. delight in the results. They all believe a strong Arafat regime is better than any possibly alternative. But it is nevertheless disappointing that international observers let themselves be used to legitimize a mockery of democracy. They did not even bother "observing" the two procedures in the voting process most susceptible to irregularities: they failed to ensure that the ballot boxes be transported under guard, and that the counting of the ballots be supervised.

Instead, they criticized Israel for having too many policemen guarding the voting places against harassment. So much for the credibility of the international community.

The Election Myth
January 26, 1996

The elections for the presidency of the Palestinian Authority and the Palestinian Council seem to have become part of contemporary mythology. Their results, widely described as the happy outcome of a democratic process, have been hailed by everyone who counts, from Prime Minister Shimon Peres to former president Jimmy Carter and President Bill Clinton. Even jailed Hamas leader Sheikh Ahmed Yassin, despite the supposed Hamas boycott of the elections, congratulated Yasser Arafat on their success. They proved that

Palestinian society was democratic, Yassin said.

These sentiments were echoed on Wednesday by Environment Minister Yossi Sarid, who told the Knesset that the government views the elections as "a great success for the Palestinian Authority, Yasser Arafat and the political process in general. . . . The elections were in effect a referendum which approved the Oslo agreements, reinforcing Arafat's position and the democratic character of the autonomy in public opinion in Israel and the world."

But a preliminary report issued yesterday by the Palestinian Domestic Monitoring Committee (PDMC), an organization of Palestinian volunteers officially empowered to monitor the elections, casts doubt on the vote's validity. Like other observers, the PDMC enumerates irregularities, including cases of ballot boxes left unguarded, gone missing, or counted without representatives of the candidates or other monitors being present. These are confirmed also by the Israeli Peace Watch observers: "Reports of unsupervised ballot boxes and papers, and of incomplete or missing polling station protocols, are numerous and widespread."

But the Palestinian monitors add to these cases a fraud no other group has mentioned: in filling their ballots, illiterate voters were assisted by relatives or agents of candidates who, as the report puts it, did not "respect the wishes" of the voters they were helping.

Had these frauds been isolated manifestations, they could have been attributed to the organizers' inexperience, inefficiency and confusion. But they fitted the pattern of manipulation and intimidation of both candidates and the press which characterized the elections throughout.

Criticisms voiced by the European-based organization "Reporters Sans Frontieres" conveyed the atmosphere in which the elections were held. The Palestinian press and radio stations, said the organization, failed to provide running coverage of the election story because they feared the Palestinian Police. Unlike the European Union's official observers, who spent a few days (mostly in the cities, not the villages) ensuring that voters could cast their ballots unmolested, the organization's representatives understood that what happened in the polling areas was only a tiny part of the story.

Confirming these charges, Palestinian human rights activist Bassam Eid said the suppression of journalists and human rights activists by the PA is "like it is in Iraq and Syria."

Regrettably, both Israel and the international community seem far less interested in the democratic process than in ensuring that Arafat's power is bolstered. But none of the post-election celebrants seems to wonder what it will be like for Israel to abut a police state "like Iraq and Syria."

The Jerusalem Negotiations
January 30, 1996

A Swedish newspaper claims that Minister Yossi Beilin, in Stockholm to receive a peace prize, will discuss the future of Jerusalem with fellow prize winner Yasser Arafat.

For four months now, Jerusalem Mayor Ehud Olmert has been insisting that representatives of Israel and the PLO have been meeting secretly in Europe, mostly in Austria and Holland, preparing an Oslo-like agreement on Jerusalem The Israeli side is being represented by the same academics — Ron Pundak and Yair Hirschfield who cooked up the Oslo Declaration of Principles. No one in the government has denied the allegation.

Prominent Palestinian activist Ziad Abu Zayyad said last week that he had participated in such meetings, which included negotiators "on the ministerial level." Faisal Husseini, who holds the Jerusalem portfolio in the Palestinian

Authority's cabinet, confirmed over the weekend that Israeli-Palestinian talks on Jerusalem are being held "to improve the chances of the coming negotiations." Communications Minister Shulamit Aloni has admitted attending such conferences, but insisted they were not negotiations, just opportunities to exchange ideas.

Yet on Saturday night, Prime Minister Shimon Peres, speaking to the convention of the Union of Orthodox Jewish Congregations of America, reiterated the traditional government position. Jerusalem is the eternal capital of Israel, he said, and it will remain undivided under Israeli sovereignty. He even assured his audience that, in Oslo, Israel made it clear to the Palestinians that Jerusalem is not negotiable. Nor does Israel have any intention of putting Jerusalem on the negotiating table any time in the future, he added.

The discrepancy between persistent reports on negotiations and Peres's assurances is distressing, but it is far less worrisome than recent developments on the ground. The presence of international observers in Jerusalem during the Palestinian election, and the complaints they lodged against the "excessive" presence of Israeli police, mean that not only the Palestinians but the world community, including the U.S., consider the eastern part of the city occupied territory. And despite vociferous government assertions to the contrary, Israel's consent to the presence of such observers constitutes a tacit admission that Israel's sovereignty in the city in is doubt.

(The government has attempted to compare Arabs voting in Jerusalem for the Palestinian Council with American expatriates casting absentee ballots in Paris for the U.S. presidency. But the notion that France would invite international observers to supervise such a vote — let alone allow anyone to complain about the presence of local police — is so absurd as to render the comparison laughable.)

Nor is Jerusalem's Arab vote for a Palestinian governing

body an isolated, aberrant development. As *Ha'aretz* correspondent Nadav Shragai has pointed out, since Labor assumed power, Israel's control of Jerusalem's eastern parts has been steadily eroding. Scores of Palestinian ministerial offices are functioning in the city despite repeated Israeli decisions to close them. Orient House operates as the PA's foreign ministry, and despite Israel's limp protests, almost every foreign minister who visits Israel pays Husseini an official call.

In day-to-day affairs, the Israeli Police is in effect inoperative in the eastern sections. It has been replaced by hundreds of the PA's "preventive security" agents, under the command of Jibril Rajoub in Jericho, who run a full-fledged police operation in the eastern city. Palestinian courts, unauthorized by Israel, resolve disputes not only among Arabs, but between Arabs and Israelis, and they have an enforcement apparatus which acts with impunity.

Despite government promises to increase public construction, Israeli building in the eastern parts has come to a virtual standstill. The Har Homa project, probably the most touted housing plan in the city's history, is yet to materialize. By contrast, illegal Arab building has reached unprecedented proportions, with the government deliberately ignoring all violations and scrupulously avoiding razing unlicensed structures.

Yasser Arafat has appointed a municipal council, which he hopes to activate in the eastern city, in competition with the existing municipality. He has even appointed a Palestinian governor for Jerusalem. The Arab schools in the city, though largely supported by Israeli taxpayers, are to all intents and purposes an integral part of Palestinian Authority's educational system.

Clearly, any relation between the government's slogans on Jerusalem and its actions is purely coincidental. Instead of the city and its environs remaining under Israel sovereignty,

Jerusalem is being surrounded by villages under PA jurisdiction. And from the little that has come out of the exploratory talks in Europe, it seems that even before real negotiations have begun, Israel is willing to forfeit control over large sections of the city and to suspend Israeli sovereignty in the Old City. It seems certain, too, that with this as a starting position, the Palestinians will have little trouble achieving the division of the city and the establishment of the Palestinian capital in its eastern half.

Unless, that is, a drastic change in government policies gives credence to Peres's brave vows.

Jerusalem Divided

February 15, 1996

When opposition leader Binyamin Netanyahu raised the question of Jerusalem with Prime Minister Shimon Peres before television cameras on Monday, Peres hastily assured him that he was wasting his time. This is not an election issue, he said. There is a national consensus on Jerusalem.

In fact, there is no such consensus even among Israel's Jewish voters, let alone in the Arab sector. And there are even ministers in Peres's government who believe Jerusalem should be "shared" with the Palestinian entity. But a majority of Israel's Jews do favor keeping Jerusalem undivided under Israel's sovereignty. And Peres, like his predecessor Yitzhak Rabin, is officially committed to the city's inviolability.

This commitment is, of course, diametrically opposed to Yasser Arafat's own commitment to the Palestinians. In every speech he makes to Arab audiences, Arafat vows that the capital of the Palestinian state, which he expects to declare within a year or two, will be Jerusalem. Anyone who does not like this, he repeatedly taunts, can drink the water of the

Dead Sea.

If the government means what it says about Jerusalem, it is faced with a serious dilemma. Peres has repeatedly asserted that making proposals totally unacceptable to the other side is an exercise in futility and a formula for an impasse. By this token, suggesting to the Palestinians that Israel remain the only sovereign in Jerusalem is a non-starter, bound to doom the negotiations. Insistence on an undivided Jerusalem is as "unrealistic," to use Labor's derisive terminology, as anything proposed by the Likud.

But if actions speak louder than words, Peres's assurances must be treated with grave suspicion. For the government's actions indicate an intention not to solidify Israel's rule in all of Jerusalem, but gradually to allow the separation of its eastern parts from the rest of the city.

A typical example of this trend can be found in what happened yesterday during the visit of Italian Foreign Minister Susanna Agnelli and the deputy foreign ministers of Ireland and Spain, known as the European Union "troika." Their official visit at Orient House after meeting with Peres was so taken for granted that Agnelli said to Peres, after he perfunctorily mentioned his objection to the visit, "No. You don't protest any more." Joining her in hearty laughter, Peres said, "Yes, I do protest."

Adopting the Foreign Ministry's euphemism, the Israeli media billed the visit "a courtesy call." But again Agnelli was honest enough to say on emerging from the building that she and her colleagues had discussed the peace process with Faisal Husseini, Hanan Ashrawi, and other Palestinian Authority officials. Clearly, virtually every foreign minister visiting Israel considers Orient House the PA's foreign ministry. It plays precisely the kind of role that Rabin repeatedly warned would bring the Oslo process to an immediate end.

Nor is Orient House the only official representation of

Palestinian rule in the city. As Mayor Ehud Olmert put it on Tuesday, "Every Palestinian Authority ministry has an office in eastern Jerusalem." The presence of these offices is not only an outright violation of the Oslo agreement's prohibition of PA activity in the city, it is a daily reminder of the government's acquiescence in this activity. Israel has all the legal means it needs, including a law passed especially for this purpose, to close these office at once. But its intent is obviously to establish facts on the ground which will assume the aura of permanence.

The government, on the other hand, is obviously reluctant to create such facts. The construction of a Jewish neighborhood in the Har Homa neighborhood in southeastern Jerusalem, in the planning for years, has been suspended. Contractors preparing to begin work there have been informed that the project is indefinitely postponed.

The picture is not all negative. The police, now opening a station in the eastern part of the city, have arrested some of Jibril Rajoub's enforcers, who operate as an independent PA police force. But such arrests take place only when the Rajoub operatives' conduct is so outrageous and abusive that even the Internal Security Ministry can no longer turn a blind eye. And while these arrests get much publicity, they have done little to stem the development of a Palestinian law-enforcement infrastructure in the eastern part of the capital.

What makes these developments particularly worrisome is that they are accompanied by Oslo-type secret talks in European capitals between semi-official Israeli and Palestinian representatives. That such secret meetings are being held has been denied, albeit not very convincingly, by the government, and confirmed by Palestinian officials. But there is no doubt that they are taking place, and that they are a telling indication of the government's long-range intentions.

Jerusalem is not, then, a non-issue, as Peres would have

Israelis believe. Whether or not it stays under Israel's sovereignty as the undivided capital of Israel is perhaps the most fundamental question before the public today, and one of the election campaign's most momentous issues.

Incitement It is Not

February 19, 1996

There is nothing unusual about the invective used in the bitter controversy over Jerusalem. The Likud's charge that Labor is conducting talks which will inevitably lead to the division of Jerusalem is perfectly legitimate, and so is Labor's indignant denial.

What is utterly illegitimate and unacceptable is to brand the Likud charges "incitement." To incite is to commit a felony. To accuse a political party of such a crime is insidious under any circumstances. To do so after Yitzhak Rabin's assassination is to associate the Likud with the murder — particularly when the charge is coupled with a sudden revelation of death threats against Prime Minister Shimon Peres, Internal Security Minister Moshe Shahal and Environment Minister Yossi Sarid.

It would be far more respectful of the public's intelligence to address the substance of the charge. That Peres is denying the very existence of talks about Jerusalem with the Palestinians hardly enhances his credibility. It recalls the time he denied the existence of his own letter to the late Norwegian foreign minister Jurgen Holst, in which he promised that the activities of Palestinian institutions in Jerusalem would be allowed to continue. The simple fact is that such talks have been taking place, that they are authorized by Minister Yossi Beilin, Peres's confidant, and that they are led by the academics who cooked up the Oslo formula in 1993. Participants on both sides have openly confirmed this.

If there is anything the government can deny with some semblance of credibility it is that these talks explicitly aim at the actual division of the city. Although the Palestinian participants seem to realize that the talks lead to the city's partition, the Israeli representatives apparently still hope to "share" the city, establishing two sovereignties in it — something they euphemistically call an administrative division — without actually cutting the city in half.

But such ideas are no more than a pipe dream. It is doubtful a city can be shared by two governments even if they are both democracies. To have a border-less sharing arrangement between a democracy on the one side and a police state on the other is unthinkable.

The Likud has an even stronger argument when it points to the facts on the ground. The government has the legal means to close down Orient House, which serves as the Palestinian Authority's foreign ministry. (Rabin once said that if Orient House became the PA's foreign ministry, the Oslo process would be summarily terminated.) Nor is this activity waning. In the past two months the PA's acting foreign minister Faisal Husseini has had more meetings with representatives of foreign governments in Orient House than in any similar period before. Yet the government is unlikely to meet Mayor Ehud Olmert's challenge to close the building by the end of the month, nor limit its activities.

Nor will the government shut down any of the other PA offices in the city, including those representing the ministries of economics, religion, health, energy, housing, veterans affairs and the water authority.

Hassan Tahboub, the PA's religion minister, emphasized the significance of the choice of Jerusalem when the ministry's office was established in 1994. "No one can deny the efforts of President Arafat's in defending Palestine in general and

Jerusalem in particular," he stated. "Therefore Jerusalem has been chosen to serve as the headquarters of this ministry." Yet Shahal last night flatly denied the existence of these offices, with the same vehemence Peres used to deny the existence of the talks.

Nor is this all. The police have arrested a couple of Jibril Rajoub's policemen acting as law enforcers in the city, and the Arab municipal council Arafat tried to revive has been neutralized. But hundreds of Rajoub's policemen are still active in the city, and courts which act as arbiters in the Arab community and in cases involving Arabs and Israelis are still functioning. And, as former O.C. northern command Yitzhak Mordechai pointed out last night, the government has halted all Jewish construction in the eastern part of the city, while Arab construction, both legal and illegal, is proceeding without government interference.

The Likud's charge is eminently pertinent. Too many signs indicate that Labor is unlikely to let the Jerusalem issue become an obstacle in reaching a final status agreement with the PLO. And Israelis must have an opportunity to decide, without being threatened with charges of incitement, if dividing Jerusalem is a price they are willing to pay for such an agreement.

The Orient House Dilemma
February 21, 1996

The government's denials of Likud charges on the issue of Jerusalem have been uncommonly vehement. But the announcement by Internal Security Minister Moshe Shahal that foreign officials would be barred from Orient House, and foreign ministry pleas to foreign officials to avoid visits to Israel in the next three months indicate that the charges have hit a raw nerve.

Perhaps most disturbing is the evasiveness and disingenuousness with which ministers are responding to the Likud's accusations. Prime Minister Shimon Peres has asserted that the government cannot prevent foreigners from making social calls on Jerusalem residents. Faisal Husseini, he said, is not a member of the Palestinian Authority's cabinet, and as a plain resident he cannot be told not to accept visitors.

But neither the foreign dignitaries nor Husseini himself make a secret of the official character of the visits and the nature of the talks. Husseini may not have the title of the PA's foreign minister, but he serves as one. And it insults the intelligence of the public to imply that prominent statesmen make the trek to Orient House to discuss the weather.

Just as insulting is the notion that Shahal would station Israeli police outside Orient House's gates to prevent, say, Germany's foreign minister or Turkey's president from entering. Neither the government nor the opposition would want such an international incident to occur, nor does anyone believe it will. In fact, when asked if the ministry intends to take action to prevent foreign ministers from visiting Orient House, the ministry's spokeswoman said, "I don't believe so." That Shahal could therefore make the suggestion only indicates that the effects of election fever are more deleterious than hitherto realized.

Nor does it add to Israel's standing to suggest that foreign visits stop for the duration of the election campaign. In effect, it is a request to foreign governments to help Labor in the elections by sparing it political embarrassment. No one doubts that if Labor wins, Orient House will continue functioning at least in its present role, despite the violation of the Oslo-Cairo accords this role constitutes. To remove its activities from public scrutiny for three months is nothing less than a concealment of the truth.

The government also maintains that the Likud government, too, allowed Orient House to function as a Palestinian headquarters before June 1992. As one minister put it, "What was good enough for Shamir is good enough for us." But there was no Oslo agreement in force during the Likud rule, nor a Palestinian Authority ruling in Gaza, Jericho and all the Arab cities of Judea and Samaria. The role of Orient House today is to extend the Palestinian Authority's rule to Jerusalem, a role it could not play when no such rule existed.

The government can, of course, deal a lethal blow to the Likud charges. All it has to do is close Orient House. As Mayor Ehud Olmert has said, such a move will not affect the talks with the Palestinian Authority. It will only show that the government is serious in denying intentions to divide Jerusalem.

A Different Vision
February 23, 1996

One of the most disturbing aspects of the ongoing Oslo process is that Israelis, who live in an open, free democracy, must often learn of developments in the negotiations from Arab sources. It used to be taken for granted that the government, though sometimes evasive for security reasons, generally tells the whole truth, while the dictatorial Arab regimes can almost always be counted on to conceal and prevaricate.

It is not that the Arab regimes, and Yasser Arafat in particular, have stopped lying. But the government seems far less open and honest than it used to be. Since Oslo it seems to be concealing the truth not for justifiable security considerations, but as a result of what can only be described as a patronizing attitude to the Israeli electorate.

As the late Yitzhak Rabin once put it, the government

"knows what is best for the people." It seems to believe that the later the public is informed about the course of the negotiations, the better. This is why Israelis first heard about the Oslo talks from PLO sources, while both the prime minister and foreign minister flatly denied that they were taking place.

Similarly, when Arafat asserted that he had a commitment from then-foreign minister Shimon Peres to preserve PLO institutions in Jerusalem and permit them to function freely — an assertion Peres strenuously denied — he was thought to be plainly lying. But in fact a letter of commitment did exist, as Peres eventually had to admit.

Two weeks ago a report leaked out of a meeting Arafat had with Arab diplomats in Stockholm. No recording devices were permitted in the room, but one of the diplomats was said to have taken down Arafat's words, and after having them translated, conveyed the text to a Swedish journalist.

The report contained statements which *The Jerusalem Post* found difficult to credit — particularly an assertion that Peres and Minister Yossi Beilin had agreed to the establishment of a Palestinian state. It was not the kind of statement Arafat would make in public, even in a closed meeting, unless he had some basis for it. and since the prime minister's office in Jerusalem called the report "nonsense," and Arafat's office in Gaza said it was "false and inaccurate," the *Post* withheld publication, even after the Hebrew press and a Norwegian paper published the story.

But now a report in *Ha'aretz* by Israel's most respected military correspondent, Ze'ev Schiff, confirms that in secret talks between Beilin and the PLO's Mahmoud Abbas (Abu Mazen) — the level on which the Oslo agreement was reached — the Israeli side had indeed agreed to the establishment of a Palestinian state.

According to Schiff, Peres has not yet decided to sign the accord, mostly because he wants the Jerusalem issue to be resolved more comprehensively, and because the Palestinian-Jordanian link which he favors is not mentioned in the agreement.

But the fact is that government representatives on the highest level have agreed to the establishment of a Palestinian state in Gaza and Judea-Samaria, with a connecting extraterritorial corridor, and have acknowledged the right of this state to bring in as many Arab "refugees" from neighboring countries as it wishes. In fact, according to the agreement, Israel will assist financially and in other ways to absorb such refugees in the Palestinian state, and allow an unspecified number to settle in Israel as part of a family-reunification program.

The plan also calls for dividing Jerusalem into an Arab "Al Quds" and an Israeli "Jerusalem," with Arab suburbs and neighboring villages incorporated into Al-Quds. The Temple Mount would be extraterritorial under Palestinian jurisdiction, and the Church of the Holy Sepulchre under Palestinian control, without being extraterritorial. The negotiators have not been able to agree on the fate of the Old City.

In the light of this agreement, Arafat's Stockholm speech does not sound incredible at all. In fact, his statement, "Peres and Beilin have already promised us half of Jerusalem," is only a slight exaggeration.

But most illuminating is Arafat's vision of what will follow this agreement, the final clause of which includes a provision that the Palestinians will have no more claims against Israel.

"We Palestinians will take over everything, including all of Jerusalem," he said. "Within five years we will have six to seven million Arabs living on the West Bank and Jerusalem. . . . If the Jews can import all kinds of Ethiopians, Russians, Uzbekians, and Ukrainians as Jews, we can import all kinds of Arabs. . . . We plan to eliminate the state of Israel and establish a Palestinian state. . . . We will make life unbearable for Jews by psychological warfare and population explosion. Jews will not want to live among Arabs."

Arafat, too, seems to believe in a new Middle East. It is just that his vision is different from Peres's.

The Terror Returns
February 26, 1996

The seven-month hiatus in suicide bombings —the longest such interval since these attacks began — led Israelis to hope that this particular scourge, if not terrorism in general, was behind them.

Some turned this hope into an unshakable conviction. In an interview with *Ha'aretz* columnist Yoel Marcus published Friday, Prime Minister Shimon Peres said, "With the Palestinians, everything is going well. All the commentators and experts who have been forecasting terrorism have proved wrong. Arafat has dismantled the PLO's own terrorist network and is fighting seriously against terrorism."

Yet the security services have repeatedly warned that the Palestinian Authority is not even trying to wage a serious war against the terrorist organizations. True, the PA has been attempting to rein in the Islamists, hoping to avoid an Israeli backlash to terrorist acts which may cause a delay in Israel's withdrawal and embarrass Peres before the elections. But it has restricted its fight to forestalling assaults. It is clearly not interested in destroying the terrorist infrastructure.

The reason offered by Arafat advocates for his reluctance to confront the Hamas and Islamic Jihad is that he desperately wants to avoid civil war. But to imply that "Arafat is doing the best he can," as Peres put it yesterday, is an inexcusable distortion of the truth. The unpleasant but irrefutable fact is that the PA is actively abetting and encouraging Hamas activities. Arafat's relationship with Hamas may not be one of warm collaboration, but it is an active, symbiotic cooperation.

No better proof of this is that Yihye Ayyash found shelter in Gaza and moved freely there, with the full knowledge of the Palestinian Police. Nor was his case an exception. Only four days ago, a Hamas rally in Kalkilya — a town bordering Kfar Sava — included a parade by intended "suicidal martyrs" clad in white sheets, and armed gunmen in black face masks. They burned in effigy a bus named Dizengoff No. 5 The rally was held under the auspices of the local PA, and boasted the active participation of Palestinian policemen.

Arafat has been conducting amicable negotiations with the very same Hamas leaders who send the suicide bombers to commit mass murder. His main aim is not that they halt terrorist activities, but that they avoid launching them from areas under PA control. The Hamas leaders seemed to have agreed to this condition, but if yesterday's Ashkelon bombing by a Hamas terrorist who apparently came from Gaza is any indication, they have changed their minds.

Peres yesterday again vowed "not to surrender" to the terrorists. It is a familiar slogan which has become a routine accompaniment to these bloodbaths. "Their aim is to destroy the peace process," he said. "But we will go ahead with our timetable." "Nor shall we relax our fight against the terrorists," he pledged. "We will pursue them without restraint."

But Israel is no longer able to pursue terrorists freely. The terror infrastructure — the bases, training camps, financial institutions, recruitment stations, indoctrination centers, propaganda outlets and arms caches — are all beyond Israel's reach now. The Oslo accords make it impossible for Israel to act against these bases. And for the first time since 1967, Israel is dependent on an Arab power to vouchsafe its security against Palestinian terrorism this side of the Jordan.

The government has imposed yet another closure on the territories. This cannot stop terrorism, but it does make the work of terrorists more difficult. Its effectiveness is mostly in that it makes the Arab population resent Hamas for causing economic hardships.

But the most effective weapon against terrorism is the suspension of all negotiations with the PLO until it shows willingness to confront the terrorist organizations. Particularly now that Israel has no access to the population centers in the territories, it must give the PLO an incentive to fight terrorism. It can provide such incentive by conditioning the continuation of the talks on the elimination of the terrorist infrastructure.

With the latest atrocity, the number of terror victims since the signing of the Oslo accords is approaching 200. It is the largest number of Israelis killed by terrorists in any 30-month period since the establishment of the state. Nor has there ever been a truly quiet period since the signing of the accords. Peres's statement about seven months of calm was inaccurate. The only thing that did not happen in the seven months since last August is a major suicide operation. In Gaza and in Judea and Samaria alike, there is hardly a day without a terrorist act, though fortunately most are unsuccessful. Even in this Orwellian age, Israel cannot go on for long believing that peace and terrorism are compatible.

Disappointing Speech

February 27, 1996

If Prime Minister Shimon Peres's speech to the Knesset yesterday was deeply disappointing it was not only for what he said, but for what he failed to say. Containing little more than a series of worn platitudes, the speech was decidedly not the kind of address the nation needed after absorbing one of the most devastating terror blows in its history.

Peres's favorite slogan is a paraphrase of David Ben-Gurion's famous World War II declaration: "We'll fight the White Paper as if there is no war, and fight the war as if there is no White Paper [a mandate from the British foreign office severely limiting Jewish immigration in Israel]." Peres's current version, initiated by the late Yitzhak Rabin, is "We'll continue the peace process as if there is no terrorism, and fight terrorism as if there is no peace process." Unfortunately, it is a slogan with little basis in reality.

Israel cannot and will not fight terrorism as if there is no peace process for the simple reason that the agreements it has signed in Oslo and Cairo make it impossible. As long as Israel honors these agreements, it cannot go after the Islamic terror organizations except in hot pursuit, and it has refrained from doing even that much.

To say, as Peres did yesterday, "No limitations have been imposed, nor will any be imposed on the pursuit of terrorists, or on the punishment of those who dispatch them, or on the destruction of their cells," is therefore unconscionably misleading.

Nor has this impotence been unexpected. The security services have warned time and again that once Israel forfeits its right to relentlessly pursue the terrorists and destroy their bases, it will have to depend on the goodwill, cooperation and efficacy of the Palestinian Authority.

Peres in effect confirmed this when he repeated the pontifical refrain which seems to follow every terrorist strike: "The Palestinian Authority must do its part. . . . I turn to those Palestinians who want peace, and ask them to prevent this violent minority from destroying their future and their hope. The ballot, and not the bullet, is the right ticket for peace and freedom."

To make his point, Peres reminded the PLO that it should feel indebted to Israel: "No people has done as much as we have to create understanding with the Palestinians. We have done this despite the terrorism."

But Yasser Arafat is obviously in no mood to shoulder either blame or responsibility, nor does he seem grateful. That he told European diplomats the Jerusalem and Ashkelon bombings were the result of a conspiracy of Israeli and Palestinian extremists betrays not only the sheer contempt he harbors for the intelligence of Israelis, but his infinite faith in the power of the big lie. Nor is this the first time he has made such a charge. Last year he accused "right wingers in the Israeli army" of collaborating in the Beit Lid massacre, which cost the lives of 20 soldiers.

Regrettably, Arafat is abetted by Peres's pronouncements when making such sickening charges. Yesterday the prime minister told newsmen that "The Hamas is like Arafat's *Altalena*, but Arafat is not Ben-Gurion." [The *Altalena* was a ship carrying weapons for the Israeli fighters in the war for independence. During British rule, Jews were forbidden to arm themselves and had to smuggle weapons into the country. Once the Israeli state was established, private military organizations were banned and the *Altalena* was fired upon by the new Israeli government to prevent it from landing its cargo.] Peres has made other invidious comparisons in recent years. He has compared the Holocaust to the bombing of Hiroshima, and the suffering of the Palestinians to that of

Dachau victims. By comparing Hamas to Menachem Begin's organization [an underground group that resisted British rule before Israel's statehood] he has given Arafat a perfect reason to legitimize the Islamist terrorists.

Sorely missing from Peres's speech was any mention of the one weapon with which Israel can still press Arafat into action against Hamas: the suspension of all negotiations until he cracks down on the terrorist organization. What Arafat wants more than anything is Israeli withdrawal from Hebron and the rural areas in Judea and Samaria, and the opening of final status talks which will enable him to declare a Palestinian state. If Peres refuses to use the one remaining "stick" Israel possesses, Arafat can hardly be blamed for assuming that he can continue to coddle Hamas with impunity.

Needed: An Unconventional Response
March 4, 1996

"We are in a state of war with Hamas," declared Prime Minister Shimon Peres yesterday, and the first question that comes to mind is how is this day different from any other? Hamas and Islamic Jihad have been waging a relentless, total terrorist war against Israel for years. In this war, they have used knife wielders, gunmen, ambushers, kidnappers, car bombs, suicide bus bombers, and even hit-and-run drivers with tenacity and imagination.

Nor did yesterday's suicide attack on a Jerusalem bus introduce anything new. The local Islamic organizations first started using suicide bombers in April 1993, well before Baruch Goldstein gave them an excuse for "revenge," and certainly long before arch-terrorist Yihye Ayyash was killed. The only difference between the more recent incidents and six attempts in 1993 (one in the Jordan Valley, one outside

Jerusalem and four in the Gaza District) is that the earlier attacks cause "only" one fatality and a few score injuries. Had the terrorists been more proficient and their intended victims less lucky, the number of fatalities could have been in the hundreds.

Why, then, was Israel's declaration of war mad only yesterday? The answer is all too obvious. Until the latest outrage, the government — trapped in a vision of a new, transformed and peace-loving PLO — hoped that Yasser Arafat would do the job for it. One of the main selling points of the Oslo agreement was that "instead of our chasing the terrorists, the PLO will do it," as the late Prime Minister Yitzhak Rabin put it. "And they will not be constrained by courts and human rights organizations," he added.

That no real peace can be attained with a regime unrestrained by courts and respect for human rights did not seem to occur to the government at the time. It was so eager to withdraw from the administered territories that it ignored the illogic of its wishful thinking. But it should not have taken long to realize that the PLO had no intention of performing the tasks Israel expected of it. Dictatorial regimes may be ruthless against internal enemies, but clearly Arafat does not consider the Islamists enemies. They fulfill the function of the shooting arm in the negotiations, something all dictatorial regimes deem an effective accompaniment to talks.

Nor did Arafat have reason to suspect that the actions of such an arm could harm his position. On the contrary. Time and again, with unseemly vehemence, Israel assured him that no terrorist act would derail the peace process. If anything, Israel would accelerate the process "to show the terrorists that they cannot budge us from our course," as government spokesmen mindlessly repeated.

The government even managed to dissuade American Congressmen who had the temerity to question Arafat's intentions from voting against aid to the Palestinian Authority. Only three days before the suicide bombing of the Jerusalem bus last week, Peres praised Arafat in reverential terms for the effective way he was curbing Islamist terrorism.

Arafat thus had all his flanks covered. No matter what his terrorists did, he was assured of continuing Israeli withdrawal and unstinting political and financial support from the U.S. and the donor nations, plus NIS 100 million a month from Israel. It was a no-lose situation. Under such circumstances, expecting him to fight terrorism and risk a civil war defied reason.

Yesterday Arafat's men averred that the incident was not the Palestinian Authority's responsibility because the bomber had come from territories still nominally under Israeli control. And while Arafat acceded to Israel's demand to outlaw terrorist organizations, he still declined to arrest the 30 terrorists whose detention Israel had demanded. It remains to be seen how effective the "outlawing" of Izzadin Kassam and the Islamic Jihad will be.

Now he may have to decide that the terrorist activity has gotten out of hand, and that it is in his interest to halt terrorist acts until after the Israeli withdrawal from Hebron and the Knesset elections. But if he hopes that Israeli pressure will dissipate in a few days he may be underestimating Israel's rage. Even Labor spokesmen, admitting that the Oslo process had deprived Israel of vital sources of intelligence, are talking of sending the army into Arab towns to liquidate terrorist cells — something they deemed unthinkable only a week ago.

Some government spokesmen even admit that by glorifying such "martyrs" as Ayyash and other terrorists, Arafat was sending a clear message to Arab youth: "The armed struggle must continue, regardless of the lip service I pay by condemning terrorist acts."

To combat terrorism, Israel is now embarked on a program of "separation" — erecting fences and deploying patrols along the Green Line. Clearly, the bombings have forced Peres to abandon, at least temporarily, his dream of an instant Benelux in this part of the world.

But fences will solve few problems. As all military experts have said, there is no way to seal off the country, particularly as long as there are 150,000 Jews living in Judea, Samaria and Gaza, and an equal number of Arabs living in Jerusalem. A total ban on Palestinian workers may help, not because it will make infiltration of terrorists impossible, but because the economic hardship it will entail may make terrorism unpopular among Palestinians.

But no defensive measure, or even Israeli initiatives against the existing terrorist infrastructure, can be effective against fanatic suicide bombers. Only inventive, unconventional means can prove effective. Promised a direct route to paradise, these Islamic kamikazes believe they must have a proper Islamic funeral before they reach heaven. It is the kind of burial of which Israel must take pains to deprive them.

Suicide Islamists were the scourge of the Sudan under British rule. The British ended the phenomenon through the simple device of burying them in pig skin, which according to the fanatics' precepts assured that they would never reach paradise. An unconventional war calls for an unconventional response.

The Awakening
March 5, 1996

In any other democracy, the events of the past 10 days would have forced the government to resign. This is not because the Labor-Meretz coalition has failed to discharge a fundamental responsibility — ensuring the safety of the country's citizens — but because it has consistently failed to tell the people the truth. In a democracy, almost any policy blunder is forgivable. Deliberately and consistently misleading the people is not.

The government has not perpetrated the misrepresentation alone. The whole world has ardently and enthusiastically participated in this Orwellian orgy of deception. Together they have named a reckless national gamble a "peace process," awarded the world's leading terrorist a Nobel Peace Prize, and concealed brutal facts and ominous warnings with cotton-candy fairy tales.

Plainly, what is going on between Israel and the Palestinian Arabs is not a peace process. The Oslo agreements, the instruments of this putative process, cannot bring peace. They are not a result of painstaking, thoughtful negotiations conducted by experts in relevant fields and submitted to national debate and deliberation. They are a reflection of the Labor government's hasty decision to unilaterally withdraw from Judea, Samaria, and Gaza.

The thrust of these agreements recalls a child's anguished cry on a Tel Aviv street yesterday. "Enough, enough, enough," she said with heartbreaking frustration. The irresistible desire to say "Enough!" to an embarrassing, agonizing, and image-tarnishing intifada was what animated the Labor government. Mindlessly, haphazardly, and recklessly, it allowed starry-eyed wishful thinkers, with little experience and virtually no knowledge of the region, to fashion a fantasy inspired by the utopian vision of a terminal dreamer. With the best intentions in the world, and catering to Israel's insatiable hunger for peace, they managed to turn a wise, scarred nation which should have known better into a jelly of gullibility.

It is a pity that President Bill Clinton, probably the most devoted friend Israel has ever had in the White House, has also fallen into this Orwellian trap. Yesterday, he portrayed the Islamist suicide bombers as "opponents of the peace process" out to undermine Yasser Arafat. If Arafat had truly opposed terrorism and wanted peace, he would not have arranged a 21-gun salute for Yihye Ayyash, "The Engineer," who dispatched suicide bombers to kill 50 Israelis, nor would he have called for a jihad against Israel, nor cite the 1974 plan to destroy Israel in phases in every speech, nor publicly lionize suicide bombers and other terrorists. Nor would he and his ministers, including the ever-so-civilized Nabil Shaath, insult the world's intelligence by blaming Israeli "extremists" for helping the suicide bombers.

These bombers and their dispatchers are not out to undermine Arafat and his regime, and they are not opposed to a process which entails Israeli withdrawal. Had they really wanted to end the process, they would have blown themselves up near Arafat and his entourage, not in downtown Tel Aviv.

What the terrorists want is painfully obvious. They want Israel to withdraw faster, from all the territories, and ultimately from the region. Above all, they want to get credit for this withdrawal. Unfortunately, they have good reason to believe they will achieve precisely that. Over and over again, with a persistence bordering on the obscene, they have been assured that no matter what they do, no matter how many Israelis they slaughter, Israel will continue "the process" and its withdrawal.

It is a terrorist's dream come true. For in the eyes of the Palestinians, particularly their young, it is the terrorists' self-sacrificing, heroic acts which are responsible for Israel's retreat, not Israel's noble determination. They believe, not without reason, that only intifada violence and the killing of Israelis caused Israel to recognize the PLO and sue for peace. If Israel continues to retreat under fire, this belief will become an article of faith.

It will be a shame if Clinton lets himself be seduced into encouraging terrorism by parroting yet again the call for the continuation of the process. What Israel needs from its friends in the U.S. is what it needs from itself at this time: to face the truth. And the truth is that Arafat will not fight fellow Arabs to satisfy Israel or even the U.S. He may put on a good show. He may manage to convince Hamas it should cease operations for a while. And he may even put some of them behind bars and use the opportunity to kill a few insignificant operatives. But he will not eliminate the terrorist infrastructure.

Arafat is not part of the solution; he is a major part of the problem. For sooner or later Israel will have to wake up and do what it should have done long ago — go after the terrorists with its own forces. At that time, it will have to face an army of 50,000 well-armed Palestinians, and perhaps a sovereign Palestinian state.

It will not be easy nor will it be pleasant. But by then, it will probably not be called a peace process.

Bravi Weizman, Olmert
March 15, 1996

President Bill Clinton's short visit to Israel yesterday was one of the most genuine and warm gestures ever made by an American president to the people of Israel. It is impossible to doubt the sincerity and genuineness of the feelings he expressed during his meetings with high school pupils and speaking on the phone to a wounded victim of the suicide bombing in Tel Aviv.

A U.S. president is never a private person. He is bound by the policy considerations of his administration as well as by the wishes of his official hosts. And it was obviously a policy decision not to hold the official welcome to the president in Jerusalem. This, despite Clinton's own pledge to recognize Jerusalem as Israel's capital and his legal commitment, through an act of Congress, to move the American Embassy to Jerusalem.

The explanation — that the president did not want to seem partial during the negotiations — is hardly convincing, since the ceremony would have been held in the western part of the city. But the Palestinian objections prevailed. As PA planning minister Nabil Shaath told the Jerusalem Arabic daily *A-Nahar* yesterday, according to the Oslo agreement all of Jerusalem is negotiable. And the Palestinians have no intention of limiting their claims to the eastern part of the city.

That President Ezer Weizman declined to accept such considerations of policy is admirable. His refusal to let Ben-Gurion Airport serve as Israel's capital was an act Israel expects of its president.

Just as admirable was Mayor Ehud Olmert's insistence on defying both the exigencies of the president's itinerary and the niceties of protocol by asking Clinton to pay an unplanned visit to the Jerusalem school which lost four graduates to terrorism. That Clinton eagerly agreed to the visit is a measure of his largeness of heart and depth of understanding. One should like to hope that, as the tough battle for Jerusalem progresses, this understanding will be applied to policy considerations as well.

Charges over Jerusalem
March 21, 1996

It is not unusual for politicians to call each other liars. And, regrettably, much of the time there is good reason to assume that the epithets are not inaccurate. Nor is it surprising that as the election campaign heats up, the contestants' lexicon deteriorates alarmingly. But the current exchange between Minister Yossi Beilin and Jerusalem Mayor Ehud Olmert is too important to be relegated to the garbage heap of campaign rhetoric. For what is at stake is the future of Jerusalem.

Some of the facts are indisputable. A proposal to divide Jerusalem, with detailed maps showing the lines of division, has been drawn up by a Jerusalem think tank as one of three options for a solution, and submitted to several political leaders in government and the opposition.

There is, of course, nothing wrong with think tanks drawing up proposals for the possible use of politicians, nor should limits be placed on their ingenuity and imagination. But according to Olmert, the plan for conceding sovereignty in parts of Jerusalem to the Palestinians was given by Beilin to academicians Ya'ir Hirshfeld and Ron Pundak who in turn submitted it to the PA minister for Jerusalem affairs, Faisal Husseini. This is vehemently denied both by Hirshfeld and Pundak as well as Beilin who has called Olmert a liar.

Under normal circumstances, such denials would have been taken seriously. But the Beilin-Hirshfeld-Pundak trio is known as the team which initiated the Oslo process. In Oslo, too, the negotiations began as one of numerous routine meetings between leftist Israeli academics and the PLO, dedicated to the examination of proposals for an Israeli-Palestinian settlement. And then, too, Hirshfeld and Pundak kept their meetings with the Palestinians secret, reporting to Beilin, who informed then-foreign minister Shimon Peres.

It is this precedent which should give Israelis pause. Obviously, during an election campaign no Labor politician will admit the party is considering relinquishing Israeli sovereignty over any part of the city. On the contrary. Speaking before the 16th annual International Jerusalem Conference of Mayors this week, Peres vowed Jerusalem would never be divided, repeating the familiar formula: Jerusalem will remain the undivided capital of Israel forever. To make the point even stronger, Beilin said on Tuesday he will head the team that will bring Moslem-Arab recognition of Israeli sovereignty over an undivided Jerusalem, an act which, he said, will render the Likud superfluous.

The trouble with such braggadocio is that it has little foundation in reality. The simple fact is that no solution except a settlement which will grant the Palestinians sovereignty over the eastern part of Jerusalem, including most of the Old City, will be acceptable to the Arab world. And even that would be deemed only a temporary step.

Nor is it reasonable to suppose that Peres and Beilin are unaware of this incontrovertible fact. This is why Jerusalem (not just is eastern part, as PA Planning Minister Nabil Shaath has pointed out) has been put on the negotiations table for the final status talks. There would have been no Oslo agreement without Israel's consent to negotiations over Jerusalem.

There is little doubt, then, that if Labor returns to power, the division of Jerusalem will become an option, if for no other reason than that Israel's refusal to consider it will cause the collapse of the Oslo process. Ironically, suicide bombings may actually increase support for such an option. While at this point a large majority of Israelis consider division unthinkable, additional terrorist strikes may make the popular desire to "separate" from the Palestinians, including the 150,000 Arab residents of Jerusalem, virtually irresistible.

Perhaps it is unrealistic to expect sober discussions of policy during an election campaign. But it would be nice if politicians who in devious secrecy cooked up the haphazard, unworkable and altogether disastrous Oslo agreement will at least have enough humility not to repeat past blunders.

An *Evening Standard* Abomination

The Jerusalem Post International Edition
Week Ending March 23, 1996

If a prize were given for the most transparent piece of disinformation planted in a Western paper, it would go to a news item in the London *Evening Standard* of February 26, a day after this year's first bus bombing.

The top-of-the-page story, whose four-line headline reads "Israeli terrorists [sic] accused of bombing" (a title the old Soviet *Pravda* would have been too timid to use), is reproduced here.

Moderate groups in Israel and the Palestinian autonomous areas were today accusing terror groups from both sides of combining to organize yesterday's bus bombings in Israel which killed 25 people and injured at least 80.

Suspicions that Israeli extremist groups linked to the military and the security services might have a hand in Palestinian suicide bombings have been voiced before, but the accusations became firmer after the assassination of Prime Minister Yitzhak Rabin.

Questioning of those accused of complicity in the murder has brought fresh evidence of connections between the groups, with the Israelis providing logistical and technical support for Palestinian bombers.

Yesterday's attack is seen as revenge for the killing of Hamas "master bomber" Yehiya Ayyash, for which Israel was accused. The following day, Israeli Premier Shimon Peres sacked the head of Israeli security, citing different reasons.

Then, too, there was speculation in Israel that the assassination was an attempt to disrupt the peace process.

Yesterday, Jewish extremists were again baying for Mr. Peres's blood. Demonstrators carrying banners reading "You are next" were at the scene of the Jerusalem bombing when he visited it.

As Palestinian police today arrested at least 25 Hamas extremists in the Gaza strip, the Palestinian Authority under Yasser Arafat — who condemned the bombing — was pointing out that even the structure of the communique issued in the name of Hamas's military wing echoed the Israeli way of describing the group rather than the usual Palestinian formula.

The Palestinian Authority also said the technology for making bus bombs no longer exists in the Palestinian areas, and the attacks could not have been carried out without outside help. . . .

In Israel, Mr. Peres was being confronted with demands from his own moderates to lift the closure of Gaza and the West Bank, which is supported by the military. Many commentators say those responsible waited until the closure was lifted in order to make sure it was reimposed.

There is no record of the story's author, Sue Masterman, in the Government Press Office. But the story's similarity to the PLO line is striking. The canard that right-wing Israeli "extremists" are partners in the suicide bombings is being repeated at every opportunity not only by Arafat, but by all his henchmen, including the Westernized Nabil Sha'ath. The *Standard* story lends the fabrication the kind of respectability only the mainstream press can grant.

Remarkably, not one source is mentioned. Unnamed "moderate groups in Israel and the Palestinian autonomous areas" is pure invention, just as "terror groups from both sides" is a fabrication.

The Palestinian terror groups are known. Hamas, Islamic Jihad, the radical PLO groups, and the "dissidents" Jibril and Abu Nidal have all killed Jews since the Oslo accords were signed.

Fatah and Group 17, Arafat's own militias, have focused on eliminating Palestinian "collaborators." But what are the terror groups on the Israeli side? Arafat has been talking for more than a year about a mysterious OAS, patterned after the French army's opponents to a settlement in Algeria.

The Algerian analogy is an Arab favorite: the French lost in Algeria and went back to Europe. And dreaming up an OAS-type group in the Israeli army which conspires with Islamic fanatics to kill Jews is a seductive fantasy.

Yet to toe this line so blindly is to disregard the most fundamental journalistic principles.

"Suspicions that the Israeli extremist groups linked to the military and the security services might have a hand in Palestinian suicide [bombings] have been voiced before, but the accusations became firmer after the assassination of Yitzhak Rabin." Voiced before? By the PLO, of course.

The connection with the Rabin assassination makes the intended impression clearer. What Masterman says is that the mad rightists in the Israeli security services who killed Rabin are now helping the Islamists destroy the peace process.

Nor does the article shy from stating there is evidence of "Israelis providing logistical and technical support for Palestinian bombers."

No such evidence exists. It is a baseless lie.

According to Masterman, GSS head Karmi Gillon was sacked the day after Ayyash was killed. But Gillon offered his resignation, quite properly, immediately after the Rabin assassination. It had nothing to do with the Ayyash killing.

Yet to a naive British reader such drivel adds a sense of conspiratorial mystery to the piece, particularly since the article then throws in the "speculation" that the Rabin assassination is connected to the bus bombings.

Having dispensed with the evil Israelis, the article introduces nice guy Yasser Arafat, who not only condemned the bombing and promptly arrested "at least 25 Hamas extremists," but also discerned that the communique Hamas issued was a forgery — it must have been concocted by, you guessed it, Israeli extremists!

All that's left is the answer to "who made the bombs." The PA says "the technology for making bus bombs no longer exists in the Palestinian areas, and the attacks could not have been carried out without outside help."

There is something truly touching about this Palestinian modesty, considering that in 75 years of terrorism Palestinians have caused the death of tens of thousands, mostly Arabs, and that explosives have been their favorite weapons.

To wind it all up, the unnamed "moderates" on both sides are heard from again. On the Palestinian side, a condemnation of the bombing. One must presume it was made by the same wonderfully moderate crowd which called "the engineer" a martyred hero, attended his funeral, fired a 21-gun salute and commemorated him by burning an Israeli bus in effigy.

On the Israeli side, the "moderates" demand lifting the closure on the very day of the first bus bombing in Jerusalem. What a felicitously quick reaction!

To add another insult to journalistic ethics, Masterman quotes "many commentators" as saying that those clever bombers and Israeli OASniks waited until the closure was lifted to commit the atrocity only to make sure it was reimposed. One can only assume that they bombed again the next week only to make sure the closure stays.

It would have been nice to believe that the *Evening Standard*, a relatively decent newspaper, would bury its head in shame for publishing such disinformation. Its new editor, Max Hastings, who covered the Yom Kippur War with fairness and later served as a distinguished editor of the *Daily Telegraph*, is not the type to countenance such journalistic abominations.

But the Masterman article was no aberration. The next week, after the second bus bomb in Jerusalem, the paper's editorial compounded the original crime with an even worse offense:

By their outrages [the bombers] *are seeking to goad the Israeli people into new acts of repression and retaliation against the Palestinians, and thus destroy the movement towards peace and compromise which is being led by . . . Shimon Peres. Hamas are being assisted in their objectives by Israel's own right-wing extremists, some of whom are prominent in the Likud.*

It is, then, no longer just OAS-type army extremists, but Likud bigwigs who are collaborating in murdering Jews.

And continuing with arrant ignorance and vicious slander, the paper states:

But at all costs the nation should avoid striking out blindly against Palestinians at large. Shimon Peres and those who share his hopes will receive no assistance, of course, from Israel's hawks. Openly or secretly, the right's long-term objective has always been to achieve the removal of all Arabs from the West Bank.

They have contributed greatly to Israel's problems, and to the rage of the Arab world, by encouraging the creation of Israeli settlements on the West Bank. . . . Shimon Peres and his colleagues deserve the support and sympathy of the western world.

The *Evening Standard*, it seems, believes it can lend such support by implying that half of the Israeli population ("the right") are Kahanists, and by accusing Likud of collaborating in the killing of Israelis.

With friends like these, Peres needs no enemies.

September 20, 1993

The Israeli-Palestinian
Declaration of Principles

Main Points

In September 1993, a breakthrough occurred in Israeli-Palestinian relations. A joint Israeli-Palestinian Declaration of Principles (DOP) was signed by the two parties in Washington, outlining the proposed interim self-government arrangements, as envisioned and agreed by both sides. These arrangements include early implementation of Palestinian self-rule in Gaza and Jericho, proposed elections of a Palestinian council, and plans for extensive economic cooperation. In addition, PLO Chairman Yasser Arafat sent a letter to Prime Minister Rabin, in which the PLO recognized Israel's right to exist in peace and security, renounced terrorism and violence, and affirmed that the clauses of the PLO Covenant denying Israel's right to exist are no longer valid. In reply, Israel recognized the PLO as the representative of the Palestinians in the peace negotiations.

1. Israel-PLO Mutual Recognition
Peace is a primary goal of the government of Israel. Since assuming power last year, the government has carried out negotiations in Washington with a delegation of Palestinians from the territories. This delegation, however, proved unable to gain the necessary legitimacy and independence in order to take the decisions and make the necessary compromises which would allow progress to be made. Throughout the negotiations, the PLO had been instructing the delegation, and the talks had, in effect, become an indirect negotia-

tion between the PLO and Israel. It was therefore decided that if the PLO would clearly show that it has radically changed its character, Israel would, in the interest of peace, negotiate directly with that organization and thus facilitate progress — provided the organization's representatives would be able to negotiate a self-rule agreement that would satisfy Israel's security interests and the Palestinians' legitimate desire to run their own lives.

2. PLO Commitments

In his September 9 letter to Prime Minister Rabin, Yasser Arafat stated unequivocally that the PLO:

-- Recognizes the right of Israel to exist in peace and security;

-- Accepts UN Security Council Resolutions 242 and 338;

-- Commits itself to a peaceful resolution of the conflict;

-- Renounces the use of terrorism and other acts of violence;

-- Assumes responsibility over all PLO elements to ensure their compliance, prevent violations, and discipline violators;

-- Affirms that those articles of the PLO Covenant which deny Israel's right to exist are now inoperative and no longer valid;

-- Undertakes to submit to the PNC for formal approval the necessary changes to the Covenant.

In addition, Chairman Arafat confirmed in writing that, upon the signing of the DOP, he will publicly state that the PLO calls upon the Palestinians in the territories to reject violence and terrorism, and to take part in the normalization of life, reconstruction, economic development and cooperation.

3. The Declaration of Principles

The Declaration of Principles contains a set of mutually agreed general principles regarding the 5-year interim period of Palestinian self rule. Many details remain to be negotiated. Also, the DOP does not decide upon issues pertaining to the permanent status, which will only be negotiated beginning the third year of the 5-year interim period. Moreover, the DOP specifically states that permanent status issues, such as Jerusalem, refugees, settlements, security arrangements and borders are to be excluded from the interim arrangements. The DOP also states that the outcome of the permanent status talks should not be prejudged or preempted by the interim arrangements, and that Israel will be responsible for the external security and for the overall security of Israelis in the West Bank and Gaza.

4. The Gaza/Jericho Plan

The DOP features an agreement in principle regarding a transfer of powers to the Palestinians, and a withdrawal of Israeli forces from the Gaza Strip and the Jericho area. Within two months after the DOP enters into force, both sides will negotiate an agreement on all aspects of the redeployment of IDF forces and on the transfer of authority in Gaza and Jericho from Israel to authorized Palestinians. Even after the withdrawal, Israel will be responsible for external security and for the internal security of the settlements and Israeli civilians. Israeli military forces and civilians will also retain freedom of movement on roads throughout Gaza and Jericho. A Palestinian police force will be given responsibility for Palestinian internal security. However, other than these arrangements, the status of Gaza and Jericho will not be different from that of the West Bank and Gaza.

5. The West Bank Interim Arrangements

In the other areas of the West Bank, five specific spheres — education and culture, health, social welfare, direct taxation and tourism — will be transferred to Palestinian representatives through early empowerment. Additional spheres may be transferred as agreed by the sides.

Concurrently, a modalities agreement regarding elections

of a Council and an Interim Agreement specifying the structure and powers of the Council will be negotiated. The elections — free, direct, and general elections — are to take place not later than nine months after the DOP enters into force. Before the elections, Israeli forces will be redeployed outside of populated areas, and after the Council is inaugurated, the Israeli civil administration will be abolished and the Israeli military government will be withdrawn. Israel will continue to exercise those powers not transferred to the Council.

6. The Interim Self-Government Council
    The Council will have executive authority in accordance with the Interim Agreement, and will be empowered to legislate within those authorities transferred to it. It will also assume those powers already transferred to Palestinian representatives in the Gaza/Jericho arrangements, and in the five early empowerment spheres. The jurisdiction of the Council will cover West Bank and Gaza Strip territory and will apply with regard to the agreed powers and spheres transferred to it. The Council, however, will not have jurisdiction over Jerusalem, settlements, military locations, Israelis or other permanent status issues.

7. Economic Cooperation
    Central to the agreement are two detailed economic annexes which outline economic cooperation between Israel and the Palestinians, both bilaterally and in the multilateral context. The vast extent of this cooperation will be directed and maintained by a joint Israeli-Palestinian economic cooperation committee. The very concept of cooperation, coordination, compatible interests and graduality of implementation are at the core of the new common Israeli-Palestinian agenda.

8. Jerusalem

Israel's position on Jerusalem remains unchanged. As recently declared by Prime Minister Rabin on the White House Lawn, 'Jerusalem is the ancient and eternal capital of the Jewish people'. An undivided Jerusalem under Israeli sovereignty is, and remains, a fundamental Israeli position.

9. Timetable

Serious negotiations lie ahead regarding the implementation of this breakthrough agreement on principles. The provisions of the DOP provide the following timetable:

A. 13 Sep 1993: DOP is signed in Washington
B. 13 Oct 1993: DOP enters into force (A + 1 Month.)
C. 13 Dec 1993: Sign Gaza/Jericho Withdrawal Accord (B + 2 Months)
D. 13 Apr 1994: Gaza/Jericho withdrawal completed (C + 4 Months)
E. 13 Jul 1994: Council elections and IDF redeployment (B + 9 Months)
F. 13 Apr 1996: Begin Permanent Status negotiations (D + 2 Years)
G. 13 Apr 1999: Permanent Status implemented (D + 5 Years)

While the above schedule is of course not final, it serves to illustrate the steps included in the DOP, which mark the path to the future Israeli-Palestinian peace.

Israel Information Service
Information Division
Israel Foreign Ministry - Jerusalem

OSLO DECLARATION

1. On the occasion of meeting in Oslo on September 13 for the first anniversary of the signing of the Declaration of Principles, Foreign Minister Bjoern Tore Godal, Chairman Yasser Arafat and Foreign Minister Shimon Peres declared their appreciation for the gradual implementation of the Declaration of Principles in Gaza and Jericho first and the beginning of the implementation of the agreement regarding early empowerment in the West Bank.

Mr. Arafat and Mr. Peres expressed their appreciation to the people and the Government of Norway for their unique role in the historic breakthrough between the Israeli people and the Palestinian people.

Representatives of the United States, the Federal Republic of Germany in her capacity as President of the European Union, Japan, the EU Commission and the United Nations were present at an unofficial meeting between the parties and the donor community.

2. The two sides declared their commitment to fully implement the Declaration of Principles and to continue the process between them based on the Declaration of Principles and on subsequent agreements.

3. The two sides declared that they see the role of the ongoing political process between them as contributing to the security of both sides and are committed to taking the necessary measures to put an end to acts of violence, moving to implement outstanding and mutual confidence building measures, promoting their economic relationship, and developing the economy of the Palestinian Authority.

4. In this context, the two sides have agreed to ask the Government of Norway, as chair of the Ad Hoc Liaison Committee, to convene an unofficial emergency meeting as soon as possible in Paris to be guided by the following principles and needs:

a. The two sides call on the donor community to make an immediate effort to meet the recurrent costs of the Palestinian Authority and the early empowerment.

b. Both sides accept the request by the AHLC chairman that they shall not bring before the donor community (the AHLC or the Consultative Group) those political issues that are of disagreement between them. They will deal with such issues between themselves, based on the Declaration of Principles and subsequent agreements.

c. The PLO reaffirms its commitment to develop the tax collection system of the Palestinain Authority in order to limit the timetable for foreign assistance to cover recurrent costs. Donor contributions to finance recurrent costs will gradually decrease with the increase of Palestinian revenues.

d. The emergency financial needs, including existing arrears, of the Palestinian Police should be financed by the donor community preferably until the end of 1994 only (and not exceeding the end of March 1995).

   Mr. Arafat and Mr. Peres will together approach the Secretary- General of the United Nations to request that the United Nations Development Programme should serve as the mechanism for immediately channeling existing funds to the Palestinian Police.

e. The parties have decided that, based on donor contribu
    tions, they will sign an understanding setting out the re
    sponsibilities of the donors, Israel and the Palestinian Au
    thority at next week's meeting of the AHLC, concerning
    financing of the early empowerment based on Palestin
    ian-Israeli cooperative efforts to establish a fully-function
    ing Palestinian tax collection mechanism. A draft under
    standing will be distributed among the donors prior to the
    meeting.

f. Subsequently, regarding the operation of the Holst Fund,
    the United States, Norway, the United Nations and others
    will commence a high level and intensive effort to gener
    ate funds and to reallocate existing funds. The United
    States has informed the parties that it will dispatch en
    voys to various capitals, including those in the region.
    Donors have advised that they will make a great effort to
    contribute to the Holst Fund and other recurrent cost in
    struments.

g. A special effort will be made to seek support for transi
    tional projects and short-term job creation projects which
    donors can implement quickly.

h. The successful implementation of the above efforts to
    cover the urgent needs of the Palestinian Authority, the
    Palestinian Police and early empowerment will enable the
    donor community to focus on the longer-term develop
    ment needs of Gaza and the West Bank.

i. In order to encourage fast implementation of Palestinian
    project development in the West Bank, the Civil Admin
    istration and PECDAR will discuss their means of coop
    eration under the existing system and procedures until full

empowerment in the West Bank is reached.

5. Mr. Arafat and Mr. Peres expressed their satisfaction with the recent positive developments in the peace process, including the recent developments between Jordan and Israel, the recent statements by Syria and by Israel and the upcoming Casablanca conference.

Chairman   Foreign Minister   Foreign Minister
Yasser Arafat   Bjoern Tore Godal   Shimon Peres

Israel Information Service
Information Division
Israel Foreign Ministry - Jerusalem

The PLO Charter *

(Adopted in 1964 and revised in 1968.)

This Covenant will be called "The Palestinian National Covenant" (*Al-Mihaq Al-Watani Al-Filastini*).

Article 1

Palestine is the homeland of the Palestine Arab people and an integral part of the great Arab homeland, and the people of Palestine is a part of the Arab Nation.

Article 2

Palestine with its boundaries that existed at the time of the British Mandate is an integral regional unit.

Article 3

The Palestinian Arab people possesses the legal right to its homeland, and when the liberation of its homeland is completed it will exercise self-determination solely according to its own will and choice.

Article 4

The Palestinian personality is an innate, persistent characteristic that does not disappear, and it is transferred from fathers to sons. The Zionist occupation, and the dispersal of the Palestinian Arab people as result of the disasters which came over it, do not deprive it of its Palestinian personality and affiliation and do not nullify them.

Article 5

The Palestinians are the Arab citizens who were living permanently in Palestine until 1947, whether they were expelled from there or remained. Whoever is born to a Palestinian

Arab father after this date, within Palestine or outside it, is a Palestinian.

Article 6

Jews who were living permanently in Palestine until the beginning of the Zionist invasion will be considered Palestinian.

Article 7

The Palestinian affiliation and the material, spiritual and historical tie with Palestine are permanent realities. The upbringing of the Palestinian individual in an Arab and revolutionary fashion, the undertaking of all means of forging consciousness and training the *Palestinian*, in order to acquaint him profoundly with his homeland, spiritually and materially, and preparing him for the conflict and the armed struggle, as well as for the sacrifice of his property and his life to restore his homeland, until the liberation — all this is a national duty.

Article 8

The phase in which the people of Palestine is living is that of the national (*Watani*) struggle for the liberation of Palestine. Therefore, the contradictions among the Palestinian national forces are of a secondary order which must be suspended in the interest of the fundamental contradiction between Zionism and colonialism on the one side and the Palestinian Arab people on the other. On this basis, the Palestinian masses, whether in the homeland or in places of exile (*Mahajir*), organizations and individuals, comprise one national front which acts to restore Palestine and liberate it through armed struggle.

Article 9

Armed struggle is the only way to liberate Palestine and is

therefore a strategy and not tactics. The Palestinian Arab people affirms its absolute resolution and abiding determination to pursue the armed struggle and to march forward toward the armed popular revolution, to liberate its homeland and return to it, [to maintain] its right to a natural life in it, and to exercise its right of self-determination in it and sovereignty over it.

Article 10

Fedayeen action forms the nucleus of the popular Palestinian war of liberation. This demands its promotion, extension and protection, and the mobilization of all the mass and scientific capacities of the Palestinians, their organization and involvement in the armed Palestinian revolution, and cohesion in the national (*Watani*) struggle among the various groups of the people of Palestine, and between them and the Arab masses, to guarantee the continuation of the revolution, its advancement and victory.

Article 11

The Palestinians will have three mottoes: National (*Wataniyya*) unity, national (*Qawmiyya*) mobilization and liberation.

Article 12

The Palestinian Arab people believes in Arab unity. In order to fulfill its role in realizing this, it must preserve, in this phase of its national (*Watani*) struggle, its Palestinian personality and the constituents thereof increase consciousness of its existence and resist any plan that tends to disintegrate or weaken it.

Article 13

Arab unity and the liberation of Palestine are two complementary aims. Each one paves the way for realization of the other. Arab unity leads to the liberation of Palestine, and the liberation of Palestine leads to Arab unity. Working for both goes hand in hand.

Article 14

The destiny of the Arab nation, indeed the very Arab existence, depends upon the destiny of the Palestine issue. The endeavor and effort of the Arab nation to liberate Palestine follows from this conncction. The people of Palestine assumes its vanguard role in realizing this sacred national (*Qawmi*) aim.

Article 15

The liberation of Palestine, from an Arab viewpoint, is a national (*Qawmi*) duty to repulse the Zionist, imperialist invasion from the great Arab homeland and to purge the Zionist presence from Palestine. Its full responsibilities fall upon the Arab nation, peoples and governments, with the Palestinian Arab people at their head.

For this purpose, the Arab nation must mobilize its military, human, material and spiritual capabilities to participate actively with the people of Palestine. They must, especially in the present stage of armed Palestinian revolution, grant and offer the people of Palestine all possible help and every material and human support, and afford it every sure means and opportunity enabling it to continue to assume its vanguard role in pursuing its armed revolution until the liberation of its homeland.

Article 16

The liberation of Palestine, from a spiritual viewpoint, will prepare an atmosphere of tranquility and peace for the Holy Land, in the shade of which all the holy places will be safeguarded, and freedom of worship and visitation to all will be guaranteed, without distinction or discrimination or race, color, language or religion. For this reason, the people of Palestine looks to the support of all the spiritual forces in the world.

Article 17

The liberation of Palestine, from a human viewpoint, will restore to the Palestinian man his dignity, glory and freedom. For this [reason], the Palestinian Arab people looks to the support of those in the world who believe in the dignity and freedom of man.

Article 18

The liberation of Palestine, from an international viewpoint, is a defensive act necessitated by the requirements of self-defense. For this reason, the people of Palestine, desiring to befriend all peoples, looks to the support of the states which love freedom, justice and peace in restoring the legal situation to Palestine, establishing security and peace in its territory, and enabling its people to exercise national (*Wataniyya*) sovereignty and national (*Qawmiyya*) freedom.

Article 19

The partitioning of Palestine in 1947 and the establishment of Israel is fundamentally null and void, whatever time has elapsed, because it was contrary to the wish of the people of Palestine and its natural right to its homeland, and contradicts the principles embodied in the Charter of the United Nations, the first of which is the right of self-determination.

Article 20

The Balfour Declaration, the Mandate Document, and what has been based upon them are considered null and void. The claim of a historical or spiritual tie between Jews and Palestine does not tally with historical realities nor with the constituents of statehood in their true sense. Judaism, in its character as a religion of revelation, is not a nationality with an independent existence. Likewise, the Jews are not one people with an independent personality. They are rather citizens of the states to which they belong.

Article 21

The Palestinian Arab people, in expressing itself through the armed Palestinian revolution, rejects every solution that is a substitute for a complete liberation of Palestine, and rejects all plans that aim at the settlement of the Palestine issue or its internationalization.

Article 22

Zionism is a political movement organically related to world imperialism and hostile to all movements of liberation and progress in the world. It is a racist and fanatical movement in its formation; aggressive, expansionist and colonialist in its aims; and Fascist and Nazi in its means. Israel is the tool of the Zionist movement and a human and geographical base for world imperialism. It is a concentration and jumping-off point for imperialism in the heart of the Arab homeland, to strike at the hopes of the Arab nation for liberation, unity and progress.

Israel is a constant threat to peace in the Middle East and the entire world. Since the liberation of Palestine will liquidate the Zionist and imperialist presence and bring about the stabilization of peace in the Middle East, the people of Palestine looks to the support of all liberal men of the world and all the forces of good progress and peace; and implores all of them, regardless of their different leanings and orientations, to offer all help and support to the people of Palestine in its just and legal struggle to liberate its homeland.

Article 23

The demands of security and peace and the requirements of truth and justice oblige all states that preserve friendly relations among peoples and maintain the loyalty of citizens to their homelands to consider Zionism an illegitimate movement and to prohibit its existence and activity.

Article 24

The Palestinian Arab people believes in the principles of justice, freedom, sovereignty, self-determination, human dignity and the right of peoples to exercise them.

Article 25

To realize the aims of the Covenant and its principles the Palestine Liberation Organization will undertake its full role in liberating Palestine.

Article 26

The Palestine Liberation Organization, which represents the forces of the Palestinian revolution, is responsible for the movement of the Palestinian Arab people in its struggle to restore its homeland, liberate it, return to it and exercise the right of self-determination in it. This responsibility extends to all military, political and financial matters, and all else that the Palestine issue requires in the Arab and international spheres.

Article 27

The Palestine Liberation Organization will cooperate with all Arab states, each according to its capacities, and will maintain neutrality in their mutual relations in the light of, and on the basis of, the requirements of the battle of liberation, and will not interfere in the internal affairs of any Arab state.

Article 28

The Palestinian Arab people insists upon the originality and independence of its national (*Wataniyya*) revolution and rejects every manner of interference, guardianship and subordination.

Article 29

The Palestinian Arab people possesses the prior and original right in liberating and restoring its homeland and will define its position with reference to all states and powers on the basis of their positions with reference to the issue [of Palestine] and the extent of their support for [the Palestinian Arab people] in its revolution to realize its aims.

Article 30

The fighters and bearers of arms in the battle of liberation are the nucleus of the Popular Army, which will be the protecting arm of the Palestinian Arab people.

Article 31

This organization shall have a flag, oath and anthem, all of which will be determined in accordance with a special system.

Article 32

To this Covenant is attached a law known as the Fundamental

Law of the Palestine Liberation Organization, in which is determined the manner of the organization's formation, its committees, institutions, the special functions of every one of them and all the requisite duties associated with them in accordance with the Covenant.

Article 33

This Covenant cannot be amended except by a two-thirds majority of all the members of the National Council of the Palestine Liberation Organization in a special session called for this purpose.

* English translation as published in *A Place Among the Nations: Israel and the World* by Benjamin Netanyahu; New York: Bantam Books, 1993, pages 418-424.

Preface to the update

In 1996 David Bar-Illan was appointed Director of Communications for Prime Minister Benjamin Netanyahu, where he served until 1999. We present selected columns he wrote up until his illness in 2000.

At the end of this section, we've included three articles dealing with Jerusalem by Zola Levitt and Dr. Thomas McCall.

Archeology Used to Bash Israel
April 5, 1996

William Dalrymple, who used to write falsehoods about Israel for *The Daily Telegraph* and *The Spectator* ("Eye on the Media," January 20, 1995), has now moved his fabrication industry to the London *Sunday Times.* In a January 21 issue he uses a book review as a vehicle for Israel-bashing.

The review is not a critique. It is a promotion piece for an attempt by Keith Whitelam to rewrite history in a book called *The Invention of Ancient Israel: The Silencing of Palestinian History.* The attempt cannot be taken any more seriously by the scientific community than the claim that Jesus was "a Palestinian," or that the Palestinians are descendants of the Philistines and Jebusites. It is obviously written in the hope of selling insidious fairy tales to the ignorant and susceptible.

Dalrymple begins his review by stating that after "conquering" Jerusalem in 1967, Israeli archeologists, trying to find "remains associated with the Jewish temples," demolished a Palestinian girls' school "to make way for the dig." It is a typical, not-so-subtle picture of ruthless, conquering Israelis destroying a school of the oppressed and occupied just to find proof for the Jewish claim to Jerusalem.

The real offense was that the Jordanians built the school in 1960 on what was obviously an important historic site. In 1967, the school was transferred by Israel to better and larger quarters, and the building was used by the rabbinate and the archeology department offices. It was razed later, when it became clear that it was in the way of important discoveries.

But according to Dalrymple, Israeli archeologists are not only Zionist fanatics and nationalistic martinets. In their feverish drive to find the "Jewish connection" in the ruins, they use Israeli schoolchildren in the digs "as part of [the children's] National Service" (only Dalrymple knows what this means).

There is, of course, nothing wrong with a nation digging to discover archeological evidence of its past though Dalrymple makes it sound like a criminal preoccupation, but to imply that Israeli archeologists are interested only in Jewish finds is an obscene lie. No one has discovered, restored, rebuilt, refurbished, advertised, exhibited and guarded Christian and Moslem relics as conscientiously as Israeli archeologists.

If anything, the archeologists have bent over backwards to preserve Moslem structures, even when it meant that digging under them, which most likely would have led to the discovery of finds with Jewish portent, had to stop.

Ironically, the Moslem authorities in the city are aware of Israel's contribution to Islamic history, and the Wakf has made no trouble for the diggers, except when they wanted to dig under the Temple Mount mosques.

With obvious glee, Dalrymple states that "to the excavators' enormous embarrassment," the ruins (under the demolished school) did not date from the time of the temples, but turned out to be "a previously unknown and rather magnificent Islamic Umayyad palace dating from the 8th century." One can only wonder why those fanatic Israeli archeologists then restored the palaces with meticulous care, invited the Jerusalem mufti to visit them, and are now featuring them as a highlight of Jerusalem's archeological tour. They could, after all, have ignored the discovery and continued to dig for Jewish relics underneath.

Adding another half-truth, Dalrymple writes, "Recently, the embarrassing Arab ruins returned to the news when Israeli zealots succeeded in taking out a court injunction against plans partially to reconstruct the palace on the grounds that the structure was 'offensive to Jewish sensibilities.'" The truth is that the Temple Mount Faithful objected not to the reconstruction of a Moslem palace, but to using Herodian stones from the Temple Mount found in the same dig stones they consider sacred for this purpose.

Dalrymple conveniently forgets to mention that the Faithful lost their suit, and that the "plan partially to reconstruct" is in the process of completion. In his attempt to imply that finds of the Arab past are predominant in Jerusalem, he never mentions that the excavations in the city have revealed structures from the Canaanite, Israelite, Hasmonean, Herodian, Roman, Byzantine, Crusader, Mameluke and Turkish periods.

Dalrymple is bothered not only by Israeli archeologists, but by the Jews' nasty habit of establishing "settlements...deliberately on sites identified as having originally been colonized by the ancient Israelites 3,000 years earlier." (Notice that even the ancient Jews were no more than invading colonizers, while the Moslems who invaded the country and ravaged it in the seventh century are, by some inexplicable leap, also the descendants of the indigenous Canaanites who were displaced by the aggression-prone Israelites.) Perhaps what truly bothers rewriters of history like Dalrymple is that the Moslems, throughout their long domination of this country, built only one town. All the Arabic names are distortions of the original Hebrew.

To buttress his charge that political bias rather than scientific inquiry animates Israeli archeologists, Dalrymple quotes an Israeli critical of the establishment. His source this time is "the distinguished Tel Aviv-based archeologist Shulamit Giva." "Giva" is so distinguished that Dalrymple not only misspells her name but refers to her as "he." Like several other Israeli intellectuals, most notably Amos Oz and A.B. Yehoshua, Geva has discovered that bashing Israel is a shortcut to world recognition. In 1992 she accused the archeology establishment of being "an executive arm of an ideological movement, a nationalist and political instrument..." rather than a scientific discipline.

Geva lives in a free country, and she is free to express her opinions, no less than the Washington columnist who in the early 1980s referred to Harlem as "America's Auschwitz" a remark which served as grist for the Soviet propaganda mills. Instead of simply examining the facts on the ground, Dalrymple uses this outburst of a decidedly less-than-famous archeologist as proof of what is happening in Israeli archeology.

In fact, Bible-oriented digging in Jerusalem, which Dalrymple attributes to Israelis, characterized Christian archeologists of the 19th century. It is the Jewish archeologists particularly since the establishment of Israel who have scrupulously exposed findings for what they are.

But facts interest neither Dalrymple nor Whitelam, the book's author, both valiant warriors in the campaign to debunk Jewish claims in the Land of Israel. There is something almost hilarious in the sudden sympathy such warriors have for the Canaanites, whom the Palestinians now claim as their ancestors. "Sometimes the adjectives slapped on the unfortunate Canaanites smack of straight racism," Dalrymple complains, accusing the great American archeologist William Albright of using "neo-fascist terms" in describing the extinct tribe of biblical lore.

It is not every day that *The Sunday Times* offers a passionate defense of the child-sacrificing, orgiastic Canaanites, and it would all be quite amusing were it not part of a conscious, calculated campaign to delegitimize Israel's presence in this country. The Arabs find it difficult convincingly to portray Israel as a usurper of the land as long as the world believes there is a connection between the people of the Bible and the land of the Bible. To deny this connection, and to depict Jewish history in the Middle East as no more than an insignificant short sojourn by passing colonizers is the purpose of today's Palestinian-Arab propaganda. In the service of this purpose, William Dalrymple is always a tireless soldier.

Jerusalem at Disney World
October 6, 1999

The fiasco of Israel's exhibit at Disney World is not merely a public-relations setback. There will be millions of visitors at the Millennium Village in the EPCOT Center, and they will not see what should have been shown in an official Israeli pavilion: that there is no parallel in history to the bond between the Jewish people and Jerusalem; and that in the 3,000 years of its existence Jerusalem has never been the capital of any other nation.

Moslems, Crusaders and Britons have captured and ruled it, but only the Jews, whether in exile or sovereign in their land, have considered Jerusalem their national capital.

Nor is there any question that Jerusalem now functions as the capital of sovereign Israel. It is the seat of government, where all internal and external state business is transacted.

None of this is shown in the exhibit. Its creators, anxious to forestall Arab displeasure, produced an "inoffensive" universalist show which is an insult to history and reality. And when even this failed to satisfy the Palestinian Information Ministry and Arab-American organizations, they yielded to threats of Arab boycott, omitted a furtive mention of Jerusalem as Israel's capital, and turned the presentation into a dull parody of Shangri-La.

The result was aptly described by correspondent Nitzan Horowitz of *Ha'aretz*, a newspaper not known for overflowing nationalist sentiment. "Contrary to the bragging of Israeli officials about a victory over the Arabs," writes Horowitz, "Jerusalem is portrayed there as an independent entity, a sort of 'corpus separatum,' a separate body. Israel as a state, an authority, a sovereigntyis not mentioned. The words 'State of Israel' are never heard or seen. Even the modest sponsorship plaque states nothing more than 'Foreign Ministry' in English and Hebrew. 'Of which country?' asked MK Ruby Rivlin."

The desire to avoid offense reaches ludicrous proportions. In a biblical scene, Abraham is asked to sacrifice an anonymous son. You want to know what Aziz of Jerusalem thinks his name is? Press a button on the computer and Aziz will tell you: it's Ishmael.

And what is the most appropriate scene with which to open a film on this modern capital city of more than 600,000, which has had a Jewish majority for 150 years? Why, the Arab market in the Old City, of course. The Knesset, on the other hand, seen from a passing helicopter, is just another building with neither name nor function. It may, after all, hurt some people's feelings to know that the seat of Israel's democratic institutions is located in (gasp) Jerusalem.

Perhaps most humiliating is that the 40 Israeli guides have been instructed to answer questions about Jerusalem's status by saying, "Israel claims that Jerusalem is its capital." This, lest we forget, is not a UN exhibition. It is an Israeli show, in which the Israeli government invested $1.8 million. That Arab organizations and governments can demand and get the right to censor it is a measure of Arab arrogance, Israeli timidity, and Disney's double standard. Such treatment of any other sovereign nation's exhibit would be unthinkable, intolerable and unacceptable.

Nor does it make business sense. The purchasing power of the would-be Arab boycotters is relatively negligible, while the disgust for Disney among Israel's friends may have a more lasting effect. It took Ford many years to overcome the damage to the company caused by Henry Ford's antisemitism.

As *Ha'aretz* put it, it is a show French diplomats would enjoy. So would the Arab regimes, despite their protests which bespeak an appetite whetted by the taste of continued appeasement.

But Jews will find it difficult to disagree with ADL national director Abraham Foxman, who, observing that Jerusalem is depicted as the capital of the Millennium rather than of Israel said, "Shame on Mickey, shame on Disney, shame on [Disney President] Eisner." He could have added, "Shame on the Jewish community leaders for letting this happen." And yet the most unfortunate aspect of this story is not that a company anxious to avoid controversy surrendered to the kind of extortion only dictatorial, bigoted regimes can practice. What makes this a particularly sad event is that it exposes the unbearable ease with which Israel can relinquish the most cherished elements of its patrimony. Such "public relations" concessions, meant merely to placate others, all too often become Israel's received wisdom. And if recent history is any guide, letting Arab threats and Disney cowardice dictate the showing of Jerusalem as a "corpus separatum" does not bode well for Israel's resilience in the coming battle for its capital.

Fighting the Last War
October 20, 1999

The scene last week could have been straight out of Herzl's *Altneuland*.

The occasion was the dedication of a Jewish school in Vienna founded by Ronald Lauder, head of the Jewish National Fund and chairman of the Conference of Presidents of Major American Jewish Organizations, and the speaker was Austria's Chancellor Viktor Klima.

Trying to assuage his audience's concern about Joerg Haider's election success, Klima told them he had called Israel's Prime Minister Ehud Barak to assure him that history would not repeat itself in Austria. Haider may be a nasty demagogue, but the large vote he received indicated anti-establishment and xenophobic sentiment, not the return of Nazism, he averred.

The speech was, at least to some in the audience, an historic affirmation of Herzl's dream in the very city which a century ago so derisively mocked the idea of a Jewish State. For, clearly, had there not been a strong Jewish state whose friendship and goodwill Austria wants, such an appearance by the Austrian prime minister would have been unthinkable.

But the official Israeli reaction to the Austrian vote, which Klima was so eager to address, would have been more credible had it been more consistent; if in the past Israeli foreign ministers had threatened severing diplomatic relations every time an election victory was won by one of Europe's Communist parties, which posed a far greater post-World War II danger to Israel and the Jewish people than the marginal neo-Nazis. In today's world, David Levy's threats betray a proclivity for fighting the last war, rather than deterring the next.

Not that antisemitism has disappeared in Europe. It has not, and there is little chance that it will in the foreseeable future. Nor is fierce vigilance ever superfluous. But it is one thing for a quarter of the population to believe, as they do in Austria, that "the Jews have too much influence," and quite another for governments to foment antisemitism. Only the state can mobilize the passions of bigotry and turn them into a genocidal threat. And today the only regimes that officially and openly promote and propagate antisemitism are not in Europe, but in the Middle East.

In Syria, Defense Minister Mustafa Tlass prides himself on a book he wrote about how Jews use the blood of Christian children in matza. *The Protocols of the Elders of Zion* and Hitler's *Mein Kampf* are best sellers there, and in the rest of the Arab world.

In Egypt's official press Jews are caricatured the way they were in Hitler's *Der Sturmer*: as slimy, hook-nosed, greedy, malevolent monsters whose blood-drenched tentacles control the world's power centers. And all the sickening antisemitic canards, from Holocaust denial to equating Jews with Nazis and charging Israeli scientists with spreading

AIDS among Arabs, are featured regularly in the mainstream press.

It is not a case of a free press gone wild. Egypt's media are controlled, their directors and editors appointed by the president. The government prohibits private radio and television channels, has shut down a weekly publication for being too outspoken, and banned more than 80 titles the American University in Cairo intended to import, including Khalil Gibran's *The Prophet.*

Antisemitic themes also dominate the controlled Palestinian media. Yasser Arafat's official mouthpiece *Al-Hayat Al-Jadida* has called chief American negotiator Dennis Ross "a Shylock, part of the oppressive racist Zionist apparatus"; branded the Holocaust "a deceitful myth"; called the U.S. Congress "the Council of the Elders of Zion" and charged Israel with trying to poison Palestinian babies. The Palestinian media also consistently deny the historic connection between the Jews and Jerusalem and the right of the Jews to nationhood.

Even more troubling is the incitement in Palestinian schoolbooks. A recent study of 140 Palestinian textbooks by the Center for Monitoring the Impact of Peace, a private foundation, shows that antisemitism is pervasive in Palestinian texts. Jews are invariably depicted as robbers, aggressors, wild animals, locusts and treacherous cheats who have faked their history and stole Palestinian land. Nowhere in these texts is there a single mention of the State of Israel or the peace agreements.

The list of the world's countries in the standard Palestinian geography book omits Israel, but includes a state named Palestine whose capital is Jerusalem. Nor do Palestinian maps ever mention Israel. All the land between the Jordan River and the Mediterranean is "occupied Palestine," to be liberated in holy war.

Palestinian officials claim that they have inherited these textbooks from Jordan and Egypt and have not managed to change them. The opposite is true. During Israel's rule in the territories, the antisemitic passages were expunged. The Palestinians restored them.

This kind of brainwashing in the media and the classroom cannot be viewed merely as a gross violation of all Arab-Israel agreements. It is a calculated, all-encompassing indoctrination campaign, a transparent preparation for war.

CNN: It's News to Me
November 5, 1999

An amusing phenomenon in the media business is CNN's claim to fairness in its coverage of Israel. There are certain things the network probably cannot help. It should not be held responsible, for instance, for the palpable hostility on its reporters' faces when they talk to Jewish residents of Judea and Samaria, those unspeakable "settlers."

Nor can the network be blamed for the arrant ignorance displayed by its Israel bureau chief about the history of Jerusalem. One can attribute his contempt for facts to trendy relativism and multi-culturalism, which have substituted political correctness for historic accuracy. After all, if *National Geographic* can publish childish nonsense about the Canaanite origins of the Palestinian Arabs, there is no reason why CNN should avoid insulting the intelligence of its viewers.

But the network does have to take responsibility for acting like the propaganda arm of Israel's extreme left and the

Palestinian Information ministry (the two are seldom distinguishable).

Example: When Binyamin Netanyahu was prime minister, CNN would invite mostly leftist, anti-government guests to appear on its programs. The excuse was that the government view was amply represented by the prime minister and his spokesmen.

But the same criteria do not apply now. In the past three months (beginning August 1 and ending October 27) not one spokesman of the opposition was invited to appear in a CNN telecast. Not one. Altogether there have been 47 guest appearances by Israelis during this period. Of these, 45, which included six appearances by Ehud Barak and nine by Haim Ramon, ranged from left of center to the extreme left (Yossi Beilin, Ran Cohen, Shlomo Ben-Ami, Leah Tsemel). Only one guest, Eliezer Waldman, who appeared twice, could be described as right of center, though he too is a member of the ruling coalition. During the same period, the Palestinians and other Arabs appeared 39 times.

This kind of bias is even more disturbing on the CNN Internet website.

Unlike a quickly forgotten news story, an archival website is a permanent fixture, a primary source of information for researchers. It has the authority of a reference library.

To peruse the CNN archive is to realize that facts no longer exist as independent entities. Like trendy "docu-fiction" novels, which incorporate real personalities and actual events into a fictional narrative, the political "profiles" section of the CNN website includes only facts compatible with the portraits CNN wishes to paint.

According to CNN, Cairo-born Yasser Arafat devoted his teen years to "a study of Jewish life, associating with Jews and reading the works of Zionists such as Theodor Herzl."

One can only wonder where in the Cairo of 1946 Arafat found Arabic translations of Zionist writings (he spoke no other language). Perhaps they were distributed by the Moslem Brotherhood as Samizdat.

These writings must have had a positive impact on young Arafat, for in the mid 1950s he and others formed Fatah, "dedicated to reclaiming Palestine for the Palestinians."

There is an unintended poignancy to this sentence. It was indeed in those years that the Arab leadership realized how much more effective they could make their efforts to "throw the Jews into the sea" if they became Palestinians rather than Arabs.

By then, the Jews of this country (the only people called Palestinians before the War of Independence) were named Israelis. Even *The Palestine Post* became *The Jerusalem Post*. By adopting the name "Palestinians" the Arabs succeeded in converting the Arab-Israeli conflict from a war of annihilation against the Jewish population to a struggle of dispossessed natives against colonialist invaders. It was a spectacularly effective canard, eventually adopted by Israel's own fiction weavers, the "new historians."

One can only wonder what turn history would have taken had King Abdullah I of Jordan not been prevented by the British from calling his kingdom Palestine. Or if Israel's founding father had heeded the advice of a young American journalist (whose name, ironically, is Sidney Zion), and called the new Jewish State Palestine.

CNN's Arafat may have been a Zionist scholar, but "his activities troubled Jordan's King Hussein," the website tells us. The activities themselves, blowing up hijacked passenger planes on Jordanian soil, agitating against the Jordanian government, and inviting a Syrian invasion, are left unmentioned. The innocent reader may be forgiven for wondering why the King was troubled.

Arafat goes on to win the Nobel Peace Prize, with no mention of the two Israelis he happened to share it with. (Why complicate a perfect fairy tale?) But he is not the website's only hero. Syrian ruler Hafez Assad, in whose capital CNN is eager to have an office, is almost as admirable.

After leading a bloodless coup, Assad "became Syria's president, repealed martial law, gave freer rein to the press and enacted other civil rights. International trade was liberalized and Syrians were permitted to travel abroad. He launched a five-year economic development plan and encouraged the development of private enterprise. Assad also admitted into his government representatives of opposition groups.

"In international affairs, Assad tried to improve relations with his neighbors. In October 1973, he and his close associate, Egypt's Anwar Sadat, launched a joint attack on Israel in an attempt to recover territory lost during the Arab-Israeli war of 1967."

Gasping with admiration for these sweeping reforms, readers must wonder why they have never thought of improving relations with their neighbors by attacking them.

It may be downright rude to point this out, but the CNN bio never mentions the Hamma massacre, where civil rights proponent Assad had 20,000 civilians killed, thus depriving them of at least some of their civil rights.

Nor does it include the litany of his unmatched brutalities in Syria and Lebanon. It even refrains from recalling one of Assad's unique distinctions. His is the only regime on earth that has officially commended army officers for beheading prisoners of war.

After all the praise the article heaps on Assad, it is quite unsettling to find in the last paragraph a brief reference to his support for "the violent terrorist organization Hizbullah," and to Syria's inclusion in the state Department's list of countries that support terrorism. No wonder Arab leaders claim the State Department is run by Zionists.

Earlier this month, CNN deviated from its dedication to errors, Arab propaganda, and nonsensical observations, and stated on an Internet webpage called "At a glance, facts and figures on the State of Israel" that Jerusalem is Israel's capital.

But when a new organization, "American Moslems for Jerusalem," protested, CNN instantly capitulated. The web was changed, and Jerusalem was converted from capital to "largest city," leaving Israel the only country in the world without a capital.

CAMERA (Committee for Accurate Middle East Reporting in America), an activist media watch organization based in Boston, pointed out to CNN that Jerusalem is the seat of government, whose status as Israel's capital is recognized by an act of Congress. The network's reply was unequivocal: "CNN does not recognize Jerusalem as the capital of Israel."

When the choice is between the U.S. Congress and "American Moslems for Jerusalem," CNN has no problem deciding.

The Press and Mrs. Clinton
November 19, 1999

Hillary Rodham Clinton's failure to react to Suha Arafat's speech in Ramallah last week made news around the world, but it should not have surprised anyone. Clinton has been an enthusiastic supporter of Yasser Arafat and the Palestinian "revolution" ever since she entered public life. Like many of her political associates in the U.S. and their Peace Now counterparts in Israel, she perceives the PLO not as a vanguard in the war against Israel's existence but as a true liberation movement.

Serving as chairwoman of the New World Foundation in the 1980s, Clinton directed contributions to PLO-affiliated groups. In the White House she entertained pro-Hamas American-Moslem groups, received gifts from them and spoke at their functions. Her advocacy of a Palestinian state in May 1998 was surprising only because it exposed the administration's true sympathies and undermined its position as honest broker.

Nor is Clinton alone in her pro-Palestinian "tilt."

Many in the American media, and practically all mainstream Israeli journalists, not to mention the trendy "new historians," are her kindred souls. Even former Labor hawks now feel, like her, more comfortable with the corrupt, despotic, and ruthless leadership of the Palestinian Authority than with the "settlers" or the haredim.

Only against this background can one understand the Ramallah incident and the dismal failure of the media to fathom its meaning.

The cold facts of the incident were plain enough. Clinton went to Ramallah to avoid making the impression that the trip was an election exercise aimed at pandering to the New York Jewish vote. The visit, billed as "official" and subsidized by the American taxpayer, had to be balanced.

Mrs. Arafat greeted her with a speech prepared by Yasser Arafat's office. It contained vicious, baseless, and irrational charges against Israel that amounted to a blood libel. Suha Arafat said that Israel used poison gas against the Palestinian population, which caused the death of women and children from cancer and other horrible diseases, and that Israel poisoned 80 percent of the water used by Palestinians, which also caused widespread disease.

Clinton had her earphones on, listening to the simultaneous translation. As Arafat began reciting Israel's genocidal crimes, Clinton nodded in approval. Then her face froze into a polite smile. When Arafat finished, she hugged and kissed her, uttering not one word of criticism. Only after the White House alerted her to the unfavorable reaction to her conduct did she issue a statement. It did not refer to Suha Arafat but commended President Clinton's plea to all sides (including the U.S.!) to refrain from provocative statements.

Clinton later explained the delay in her reaction by stating that the simultaneous translation was "unclear" and "incomplete."

But most of the journalists present listened to the same translation, and they all clearly heard Arafat's charges. *Reuters* correspondent Deborah Camiel was particularly accurate in her report, but most other reporters, too, seemed to have no trouble with the translation. Correspondents for CNN, *The New York Times, The Washington Post, The New York Post, Knight Ridder*, and others got it right.

To be sure, some reporters tried to help Arafat by explaining that she probably meant tear gas, not poison gas, and others tried to help Clinton by reporting that she sharply rebuked Arafat when in fact she never referred to her by name.

If there was any serious distortion, it appeared in newspapers that drastically edited the wire service reports to suit their politics.

The International Herald Tribune, for example, published a drastically curtailed AP story which described Clinton's statement from Petra the next morning not as a response to the Arafat speech but as criticism of "Palestinian officials" for "pushing the issue of statehood into the spotlight."

The first reference to the speech came only in the fourth paragraph: "Suha Arafat...used a speech introducing Mrs. Clinton to criticize environmental and health damage that, she asserted, had been caused by tear gas and other means to control crowds during Israel's occupation of Palestinian lands."

The story even distorted the Israeli reaction, describing it merely as "saying such issues should be placed on the negotiating table."

It ignored the government's statement that such comments have "no connection to reality" and that they "poison the public atmosphere." Saeb Erekat could not have given it a better spin.

But while the distortion and omission of facts was minimal, most reporters tried to control the damage by giving Arafat's remarks an environmental spin.

After all, almost everyone is guilty of pollution: from smokers who disregard the health hazard they pose to others, to industrial plants that contaminate rivers with chemicals.

In turning this spin, foreign journalists were helped by *Ha'aretz*, which headlined its front-page story "Suha Arafat: Israel polluted air and ground in the territories."

Environment Minister Dalia Itzik unintentionally reinforced this impression by inviting Suha Arafat to inspect the incalculable environmental damage caused not by Israelis but by the reckless and anarchic practices of the Palestinian Authority.

Only a few in the media realized that what Arafat said had nothing to do with environmental pollution. Among them were *The New York Post, Washington Post* columnist George Will (appearing on ABC-TV's *This Week* on Sunday), *New York Daily News* columnist Sidney Zion, and *Washington*

Times columnist Cal Thomas.

Unlike most other journalists, they understood that Suha Arafat's speech was just the latest installment in a systematic, calculated Palestinian campaign of blood libels.

The Zionist Organization of America has compiled a litany of these libels. Following are a few examples:

On March 16, 1997, Yasser Arafat's representative to the UN in Geneva, Nabil Ramlawi, lodged a formal complaint accusing "the Israeli authorities" of injecting 300 Palestinian children with the HIV virus.

In June of that year, Abdel Hamid al-Qudsi, deputy minister of the PLO's Palestinian Authority Ministry of Supplies, declared: "Israel is distributing food containing material that causes cancer and hormones that harm male virility and also spoiled food products in the Palestinian Authority's territories in order to poison and harm the Palestinian population.

"We absolutely feel that it is an organized plan and conspiracy which is under the auspices of the Israel Defense Forces. This is a planned and initiated war against the Palestinian people."

Six months later, Maher al-Dasouqi, director of the Palestinian Authority's Committee for Consumer Protection, declared in Arafat's official newspaper, *Al- Hayat Al- Jadida*: "Citizens must be vigilant regarding chocolate from England, especially Cadbury's, which is very popular in Palestinian markets, since the milk used in the production of all types of [Cadbury's] chocolate was infected with mad-cow disease.

"The sale of this chocolate is forbidden in England, but it was smuggled into the Palestinian regions by Israeli merchants...."

Last year, the same paper quoted Arafat's consumer-protection chief: "Israel floods our markets with hundreds of thousands of food products unfit for human consumption...the purpose of which is to spread disease, debility, and slow death in the Palestinian body.... Children are the main target of this plan."

Only last week, on November 9, *Al-Hayat Al-Jadida* charged that "Israeli chemical companies are using the Palestinians and their land for experiments...deciding according to the results if these chemicals should be marketed in Israel."

And commenting on Suha Arafat's speech in *Al Hayat* this week (November 15), columnist Fuad Abu Hadjla wrote: "We understand the American position...in defending Israel and its right to oppress our people and murder them with poison gas, since these gases and most of the murderous Zionist technologies originate in American industry."

To pinpoint the progenitor of these blood libels, it would be necessary to go back to the Middle Ages, when Jews were accused of causing the Black Death by poisoning the wells.

But the media have deliberately ignored this campaign of antisemitic incitement. The charitable explanation is that they have sacrificed truth and professional integrity for the sake of the peace process. It is probably also the excuse for failing to put the Suha Arafat story in context.

The media have even failed to notice that the PA, refusing to apologize to Israel, proffered an apology only to Hillary Clinton, not for the antisemitic calumny, but for any embarrassment the speech might have caused her.

The press is not alone in this obtuseness. Neither the Israeli government nor the administration seems willing to recognize that the only governments that propagate and encourage antisemitism today are the Arab regimes. For some unfathomable reason, these regimes are never criticized, let alone censured, for a crime deemed totally unacceptable by civilized society.

Is there a racist double standard at play? Are Arab regimes expected to act as if they are living in the Middle Ages?

Are they too immature to be held responsible for their actions?

To answer these questions all one has to do is imagine the reaction in Israel and abroad had Suha Arafat's words been uttered by, say, Joerg Haider or Pat Buchanan.

Greatest Story Never Told
November 26, 1999

An article of faith shared by virtually all the media is that the Palestinian body politic is divided: the majority are pro-peace moderates, supporters of Yasser Arafat and the PLO, opposed by anti-peace extremists, followers of the Islamist Hamas. And since most journalists seem to feel their mission in life is not just to report the news but to help the cause of peace, the result is inevitable. They minimize or ignore news that may harm Arafat and the PLO, and bash their opponents. Like all Western governments, they are convinced that if Arafat is weakened the extremists will prevail, Hamas will take over, and the hope for peace will vanish.

The only trouble is that the premise of this theory is false. The simplistic good guys-bad guys division is divorced from reality.

A study soon to be published by the Palestinian Media Watch confirms what observers of the Palestinian scene have known for a long time: The differences between the PA and Hamas are over the role of religious law in society and government, and over who should be in power. There are no differences on issues related to Israel.

Both the PA and Hamas deny Israel's legitimacy, both define Israel as the occupying power of "all of Palestine," including the area currently known as the State of Israel, and both want the elimination of Israel as a sovereign Jewish state.

Nor do they attempt to conceal the commonality of their purpose. True, the Islamists believe that the Oslo agreement retards and inhibits Palestinian mobilization against Israel, and that only a relentless armed struggle can achieve Israel's destruction. And the more pragmatic Arafat views Oslo as the first stage in "the plan of stages" formulated by the PLO in 1974, which advocates the use of diplomacy as well as violence in an incremental war against Israel. But the ramifications of these disagreements are strictly tactical.

As the Palestinian Media Watch study demonstrates, the similarity between Hamas doctrine and PA rhetoric is striking. PA Communications Minister Immad Falouji, himself a Hamas member, summed up the common goal only last week in the PA official newspaper *Al Hayat Al Jadida* (November 18).

"Our nation is full of hope for the future. The occupying power will not continue to exist, no matter how powerful and arrogant it may be," he said.

Four days before, Chief of Preventive Security in Gaza Muhammad Dahlan made clear that the argument with the Hamas was solely over tactics.

"We believe that military action at this stage definitely does not serve the national interest, which is why we shall not permit action motivated by emotion." (*Al Hayat Al Jadida*, November 14.)

It is instructive to compare the formulations of the Hamas covenant with the language used in sermons by PA-appointed imams. The covenant states that "Palestine is Islamic Wakf (sacred) land, for all generations of Moslems until Judgment Day."

It declares that "the liberation of Palestine is the duty of every Moslem wherever he may be," and that no one is permitted to "abandon or concede any part of Palestine, the robbery of Palestine by the Jews makes Jihad imperative."

In his sermon on April 30, Yusef Abu Sneineh, the PA's imam whose sermons are broadcast on *The Voice of Palestine,* made identical assertions: "The land of Palestine is Wakf land for all Moslems, east and west. The liberation of Palestine is the duty of all the peoples of Islam, not only the Palestinian people. The land of Moslem Palestine is one unit, indivisible. There is no difference between Haifa and Nablus, Lod and Ramallah, Jerusalem and Nazareth. There is no religious sanction for dividing Palestine into districts and recognizing the occupation. No one is allowed to give it up or divide it."

Arafat himself has often emphasized the inevitability of Jihad. He told his newspaper *Al Hayat Al Jadida* in January, "The agreements will not liberate the land. Every centimeter demands a struggle, the land demands blood."

His Foreign Minister Farouk Kaddumi said this week, "The PLO weapons in Lebanon are for continuing the struggle in all ways when necessary: the political process does not seem to promise a just solution."

Nor does the PA lag behind the Hamas in expressions of classic antisemitism. The Hamas covenant decries "the Nazi Zionist practices against our people."

Al Hayat Al Jadida editor Hafez Bargouti refers to "Israeli attempts to perform Nazi massacres on us."

The Hamas charges that "[The Jews] have used their money to dominate the international media, the news agencies, press, broadcasting and publishing houses."

The official PA newspaper states, "The Jews' success is no accident. It is a result of long years of planning and huge efforts to achieve control of the world's news media."

Both *Al Hayat Al Jadida* and the Hamas covenant accuse Jews of being the force behind all wars and upheavals (specifically the French and Russian revolutions), and behind such clandestine sinful organizations as the Freemasons and Rotary Clubs. Authors of *The Protocols of the Elders of Zion*, they are the origin of all corruption in the world.

Such similarities are hardly accidental. Article 27 of the Hamas covenant explicitly describes the relationship between the Islamic organization and the PLO: "The PLO is among the closest to the Hamas, for it constitutes a father, brother, relative, friend. Can a Moslem turn away from his father, brother, relative or friend? Our homeland is one, our calamity is one, our destiny is one and our enemy is common to both of us."

Nor is the feeling unrequited. Arafat, who in his youth belonged to the Moslem Brotherhood in Egypt, has made no secret of his filial relationship with the Hamas. He embraces and kisses its leaders, declares that all Palestinians must aspire to follow the footsteps of the martyr Yihye Ayyash (the notorious "Engineer" responsible for 50 Israeli deaths who was assassinated in 1995). He shelters Ayyash's successor Muhammad Deif, and refers to Hamas's spiritual leader Sheikh Yassin as "my brother."

This week, the PA offered a home to the Hamas leaders expelled from Jordan.

Israel's intelligence agencies repeatedly assert that Arafat has no intention of confronting the Hamas or its military wing. His activity against terrorism is restricted to preventing actions that can be traced to PA territory, and even these restrictions apply only "at this stage," according to Dahlan.

Fatah central committee member Hani Hassan put it aptly two years ago: "Our unity is like a building, and we must distribute the work among the builders." (*Al Ayyam*, August 31, 1997.)

All this makes the media treatment of the Arafat story one of the great puzzles of our time. In the past 30 years Arafat has allied himself with every anti-Western and anti-American regime and organization on earth: the U.S.SR, East Germany, Cuba, the Red Brigades, Bader Meinhof, the Japanese Red Army, Saddam Hussein, Muammar Gaddafi, and the Iranian ayatollahs.

He has ordered the murder of children, the kidnapping and killing of athletes, and the execution of American and other Western diplomats taken hostage by his gunmen. Now he is a certifiably corrupt tyrant who tortures and executes real and imagined opponents at will. He identifies with Hamas, an extremist, antisemitic, anti-Western organization sworn to Israel's destruction, and he matches the virulence of its rhetoric by heaping medieval blood libels on Israel.

Yet he is celebrated and lionized throughout the world, hailed by governments and the media as an astute and moderate leader, the world's best hope for peace in the Middle East. Just to keep him happy, the government of Israel gives him a personal grant of close to $100 million a year, and the U.S., Europe and Japan make huge contributions to his regime. If he declares a Palestinian state next year, he will have the support of almost all the world's governments.

There must be a story here somewhere.

A CNN footnote: Last month, American Muslims for Jerusalem, an umbrella organization of anti-Israel groups, launched a campaign against the CNN website, which named Jerusalem the capital of Israel. The same organization had spearheaded the boycott threats against Disney for calling

Jerusalem the capital of Israel in its EPCOT Millennium Village exhibit. AMJ was also active in pressuring Burger King to shut down a franchise restaurant in Ma'aleh Adumim.

Among the constituent members of American Muslims for Jerusalem are CAIR, the Council on American Islamic Relations, and the Muslim Public Affairs Council. CAIR is a spinoff from a "Hamas front," according to Oliver Revell, a former head of the FBI's counter-terrorist investigation. MPAC is a Los Angeles-based group whose executive director, Salam Al-Marayati, has supported Holocaust-denier Roger Garaudy.

The *Cable News Network* promptly removed references to Jerusalem as Israel's capital. But after discussions with representatives of CAMERA (Committee for Accuracy in Middle East Reporting in America), the CNN web page was changed again. It now states that Jerusalem is "the seat of Israel's government and its self-declared capital, although its status is in dispute." This is essentially accurate. Hats off to CNN.

Invitation to pressure
December 8, 1999

It is impossible not to admire the tenacity and perseverance of Secretary of State Madeleine Albright, Special Coordinator Dennis Ross, and other administration officials as they once more visit the region in an effort to move the Oslo process forward.

Yet the visit's scenarios are all too predictable. Hafez Assad will say that, having magnanimously made a strategic decision for peace, he would be willing to negotiate with Israel provided all his conditions are met in advance.

Ehud Barak will complain that his many concessions, the release of terrorists convicted of murder, the evacuation of 11 settler outposts, the opening of the "secure passage," the relinquishment of another five percent of Judea and Samaria, and, above all, the abandonment of Israel's insistence on Palestinian compliance and reciprocity, have only hardened Palestinian positions.

And Yasser Arafat will say that unless the U.S. pressures Israel to stop settlement activity forthwith, the negotiations will get nowhere and violence will erupt.

At first glance, the Palestinians' demand for American pressure on Israel, dramatized by a staged walkout from the talks on Monday, seems like the height of hutzpa. Arafat's actions in recent weeks should hardly instill confidence in American hearts.

Faced with a protest by Palestinian public figures and legislators against PA corruption and oppression, he arrested the public figures and made threats against the legislators, one of whom was shot on his way home.

And as if to confirm the protesters' complaints, Arafat appointed an officer convicted of torturing a Palestinian to death as the PA's general prosecutor. His Fatah movement, whose charter still calls for dismantling the State of Israel, has issued a warning to Palestinians to prepare for a violent confrontation with Israel.

And the administration could not have been overly pleased by Suha Arafat's "poison gas" speech that accused Israel of causing cancer among Palestinian women and children, or by the charge published in Arafat's official newspaper, *Al-Hayat al-Jadida*, two days later.

"We understand the administration's defense of Israel's right to oppress our people and murder us with poisonous gases, since these gases, and most of the murderous Zionist technologies, are of American manufacture," wrote the paper's editorial columnist, Fuad Abu Hajla.

Nor can Washington be unaware that such anti-Americanism is characteristic of the PA chairman. He has allied himself with every enemy of the U.S. throughout his career. Last month he sent an adulatory message to Iraqi dictator Saddam Hussein, wishing him success in removing "the unjust embargo" and expressing the hope that together they will "regain holy Jerusalem."

Last week he invited Slobodan Milosevic to celebrate the Russian Orthodox New Year in Bethlehem.

If anything, it would have been reasonable to expect American pressure on Arafat, not on Israel. Pressure to democratize, liberalize, comply with agreements, and stop preaching violence. Pressure to extradite, as demanded by Congress, the 23 terrorists implicated in killing Americans, five of whom are serving in the Palestinian police.

But the chances of the administration seriously demanding anything from Arafat are slim. The basic premise of American policy is that Arafat is the only Palestinian leader capable of making peace, and that pressure on him may cause his collapse and destroy the process. This is why Hillary Clinton never condemned Mrs. Arafat's blood libel specifically, and why the White House demanded a Palestinian apology only for embarrassing the first lady, not for the contents of her antisemitic speech.

Unfortunately, the administration is not alone in this attitude. Ever since Oslo, four Israeli prime ministers have subscribed to the same seductive but flawed premise. Arafat is not moving his people toward peace. He is inculcating the Palestinians with expectations that even the most recklessly concessionary Israeli government could not fulfill.

At most, Israel may be able to avoid an immediate

confrontation by reaching another interim agreement, which might, just might, put these expectations on hold.

Such a deal would not only be fraught with uncertainty and unrest, it would condemn the Palestinians to life under an oppressive, despotic, and corrupt regime, a prospect the enthusiastic advocates of a Palestinian state under Arafat must bear on their conscience.

The alternative is to effect a policy change neither the administration nor Israel seems ready to make. It would require uncompromising insistence on a system of accountability in the Palestinian Authority, a total change in its education system, and active Western support for democratic elements in Palestinian society.

This may be more difficult than the quick fixes of White House Lawn ceremonies. But it is the only way to lasting peace.

A Prelude to War
December 15, 1999

What supporters of the proposed agreement with Syria expect is clear.

Once the treaty is signed, the dream of comprehensive peace in the Middle East will finally materialize. Israel and its neighbors will be swamped with investors. Tourism will burgeon. And free movement of people and goods will transform the Arab dictatorships into enlightened, advanced societies. Surely, relinquishing the Golan, painful though it may be, is not too high a price for so promising an outcome.

True, even the terminally optimistic realize that the Golan will not be the last Israeli concession. The "root cause" of the Arab-Israeli conflict, the Palestinian problem, must also be addressed. But the momentum created by peace with Syria, they believe, will persuade the Palestinians to reach a reasonable compromise.

To debunk this utopian scenario is all too easy. The expectation that, once Israel "returns to its natural size," the Arab regimes will discard antisemitic incitement, change textbooks, reduce military budgets, seriously fight anti-Israel terrorism, support Israel in the international arena, and promote peaceful cooperation instead of Israel's delegitimation is a wish-dream that belongs in fairy tales, not in Middle East reality.

As recent experience has shown, the more concessionary and conciliatory Israel is, the weaker it is perceived to be, and the more likely it is to be subjected to escalating demands. Nor is there any evidence that peace and stability attract investors rather than the prospect of profits and a business-friendly environment. Some of the poorest countries in the world are peaceful and stable.

Before surrendering the Golan, it may be useful to remember that unlike Israelis and other Westerners, whose passion for instant gratification is quintessentially summarized in the slogan "peace now," Arabs view the conflict with an historic perspective. They believe the Zionist enterprise is a foreign invasion like the Crusades, and that regardless of its current viability it is doomed to fail.

When the 1973 war made them realize that Israel could not be defeated in a frontal military attack, they changed tactics, not goals. The Arab League and the PLO constructed "the plan of stages," which envisioned retrieving as much territory as possible by peaceful means and attacking Israel only after it becomes diminished and demoralized.

In Arab eyes, the plan is proceeding nicely despite internecine bickering. Israel's gains in the 1967 war are being gradually eliminated, and the military balance is changing. Egypt, which in 1967 was a second-rate power equipped with inferior Soviet arms, now has a powerful, American-armed military force. Despite traditional American promises to maintain Israel's qualitative edge, the Egyptian army has been supplied with sophisticated arms Israel does not have.

The Syrian army now expects to undergo a similar transformation.

Ill-equipped and strapped for funds, it will be armed and trained by the U.S. And since the administration has not demanded that it withdraw from Lebanon, it will be able to threaten Israel on two fronts.

The basic premise of President Clinton's Pax Americana now being imposed on the region is that the main players should depend on American aid and arms, giving Washington control over their military moves. That in the volatile Middle East such calculations do not always work was evinced in Iran, where the vast American-built military infrastructure fell into the hands of the ayatollahs.

To make the impending agreement palatable, a campaign of purification of the Assad regime has been launched by both the U.S. and Israel. But Assad has not changed. He is a ruthless despot, a sponsor of terrorism, and a major drug exporter who has kept Syria isolated, oppressed, and poor.

Touted as a man of his word, Assad has broken virtually every agreement he has ever made with Turkey, the Arab countries, and the U.S. The only area in which he avoids trouble is the Golan, where the Israeli army is within striking distance of Damascus.

Nor is it likely that peace with Israel will make Syria "join the world." Totalitarian regimes know how to filter foreign influences.

Chances are the opposite will happen. Syria considers not

only Lebanon, but Israel and Jordan as part of Greater Syria. It is a belief deeply rooted in its history and national mystique, and openly shared by Israeli Arab leaders. Syrian free access to these leaders is almost certain to create a wave of irredentism, which will transform today's demands for Arab autonomy in Galilee to agitation for secession.

Combined with Syrian presence near (if not on) the Kinneret, the prospect of such agitation makes Syria's reoccupation of the Golan a decisive step toward the realization of the plan of stages.

And, lest we forget, the last stage of this plan is war.

It's the Height of Hubris
December 22, 1999

It is hardly surprising that Israel supports the American-British insistence on linking the removal of sanctions against Iraq to the resumption of international inspection there. No one better understands the need to be tough, distrustful, and determined when dealing with murderous totalitarians.

But this insistence on inspection, aimed mainly at preventing Iraq from developing nuclear weapons, should also remind Israelis that world consensus does not always represent fairness and good judgment. No government, and hardly anyone in the media, supported Menachem Begin's action against the Osirak reactor.

Even the White House, then inhabited by a true friend of Israel, not an appeaser masquerading as one, was harshly censorious. Only Iraq's assault on Kuwait nine years later forced the world to recognize Israel's crucial contribution to international security and stability.

Nor should Israelis forget that some of the country's most

esteemed politicians and military experts, including Shimon Peres and Ezer Weizman, vehemently opposed the action and tried to abort it.

The toughness on Saddam must also make Israelis wonder about the double standard that dominates Western attitudes to Syria's Hafez Assad. In the competition for the title of most ruthless tyrant of the post-War era, Saddam and Assad run neck and neck.

Both have massacred tens of thousands of their own people, Saddam having a slight edge in that he used poison gas to kill 6,000 of them. Both have invaded a small neighboring state claiming that it is no more than a province of their own country. Both have supported anti-Israel and anti-Western terrorism (with Assad having a clear edge), and both have broken virtually every agreement they have ever made.

Yet Assad's invasion and annexation of Lebanon has been legitimized by the West's indifference. And unlike Saddam, a despised pariah subjected to sanctions and calumny, Assad is a sought after, extravagantly praised leader. There is no parallel in Israel's history to the phenomenon of an Israeli prime minister paying sycophantic homage to a dictator who shelters the worst Nazi war criminals and whose defense minister has written a book claiming that Jews use gentile children's blood for matza.

Even more disturbing are Barak's scare tactics. Reminding the cabinet of the havoc created by Iraq's "42 antiquated Scuds" in 1991, he warned against the terrible destruction Syria's arsenal of modern missiles could inflict if the talks fail.

To say that using the Syrian threat in the debate over the Golan means surrender to extortion is to understate the case. If Israel is so intimidated by Syria's missiles, there can be no limit to concessions.

One can only tremble at the prospect of Barak's reaction if Damascus threatens to use its missiles unless Jerusalem becomes the capital of a Palestinian state and Galilee is annexed to Syria.

If anything, the Scud example should have led to the opposite conclusion. Between Israel and Iraq there is no conflict over "occupied territories" or UN resolutions. Yet when Saddam believed he could gain points with the Arab regimes by bombing Israel, he did so. His actions should have also demonstrated the value of treaties in the Middle East.

Saddam signed a nonaggression pact with Iran before invading it, and turned on Kuwait, his ally and bank-roller in that war, as soon as he thought he could do so with impunity.

To suppose that Assad will destroy Syria's missile arsenal after signing an agreement with Israel, or that he will abandon his designs on "Southern Syria," namely Israel and Jordan, is to ignore his own record of agreement violations and to underestimate his commitment to Syria's "historic destiny."

Not long ago Barak seemed to understand the difference between agreements with dictatorships and peace among democracies. When the late Yitzhak Rabin negotiated with the Syrians, Barak insisted that Israel must remain on the Golan even in time of peace.

The reason was as compelling then as it is now. As long as the danger of Syrian attack is present, and Barak's emphasis on security arrangements makes clear that it is, relinquishing a strategic asset like the Golan is reckless and irresponsible. To boast that Israel can do without this natural barrier to invasion is to display the same hubris Rabin exhibited when he asserted in the spring of 1973 that Israel was so strong that no Arab regime would dare attack it.

The only way aggression by dictatorial regimes can be

prevented is through credible deterrence. Any significant diminishment of such deterrence is an invitation to war.

Total Mobilization
December 24, 1999

If the almost total mobilization of the media to the cause of withdrawal from the Golan had not been so worrisome in a democratic society, it could have rated as the most amusing comedy of the season.

The alacrity with which almost all newsmen and commentators jumped to attention and tried to outdo each other in supporting government policy recalled the way their spiritual ancestors changed political positions according to the latest party line communiqué from Moscow.

One of the few exceptions was Emmanuel Halperin, host of Channel 1's late-night News, who interviewed Maj.-Gen. (res.) Ori Orr soon after Clinton's announcement of the resumption of the talks. Orr's smug, arrogant and altogether obnoxious manner recalled the perpetual haughtiness Israeli generals used to sport after the Six Day War.

"Was it all a fraud, was it 30 years of brainwashing?" asked Halperin, referring to the IDF doctrine that the Golan was crucial to Israel's defense. "And were the opinions of all those American generals who said the Golan was indispensable to Israel's survival completely invalid?"

Orr seemed not only to have no trouble toeing the new party line, which represents a 180-degree turn from the old, he averred that the Golan is actually a security burden, not an asset. After all, he said, we lost more soldiers defending it in 1973 than in capturing it in 1967.

It is at moments like these that Harry Truman's

unprintable opinion of generals assumes the luminosity of Confucian wisdom.

But Halperin's outspoken doubts stood out as a rare exception. Other news hosts, from the venerable Haim Yavin through the feverishly inventive Channel 2 anchors, to the intemperate Yael Sternhell on Channel 1's 7:30 Edition, could neither contain their enthusiasm for government spokesmen nor conceal their hostility for anyone who dared disagree.

To increase their bullying power, the Channel 1 crew bolstered their ranks with guest co-hosts of identical or even more dovish political proclivities.

With Aryeh Golan and Haim Baram in tow, they put on a credible imitation of the monolithic state radio in the days of Mapai, minus, alas, the nationalism that was still in evidence then. It almost made one nostalgic for the days when *Jerusalem Post* editorials had to be approved by the Ministry of Foreign Affairs.

It is easy enough to prove with statistics how lopsided the guest list is on these programs. But numbers tell only half the story. On the rare occasion that credible representatives of the opposition did appear, they were heckled, interrupted, mocked and derided by their interviewers. The only thing these would-be apparatchiks have not done is turn off the microphone when interviewees presented persuasive arguments.

But they all sounded like paragons of objectivity compared to Channel 1 star commentator Ehud Ya'ari, whose harangues were hardly distinguishable from Syrian press releases.

Israelis should understand the Syrians' frustrations, he intoned. When the talks began in Madrid under Yitzhak Shamir, the poor Syrians had to suffer the bad manners of Yossi Ben-Aharon and Yigal Carmon. (This is a reference to a meeting in which Ben-Aharon had the hutzpa to pull out Syrian Defense Minister Mustafa Tlass's book about how Jews use gentile children's blood to make matza. Slamming it on the table, he asked his counterpart, Muafek Alaf, how he could reconcile talk of peace with such antisemitic incitement.)

The Syrians first trusted Rabin, continued Ya'ari, but then he turned away from them and made a deal in Oslo with the Palestinians. Then Peres broke off the talks in 1996. And Netanyahu, too, withdrew from the back-channel negotiations just when they thought they were getting everything they wanted.

Poor Syrians! No wonder they refused to shake hands.

Ya'ari's sycophancy has become his trademark. He must believe, probably with good reason, that only by playing up to Arab leaders will he get exclusive interviews with them. But to exonerate Assad and blame Israel for the failure of the negotiations in 1991-1999 is the kind of groveling that crosses the line of the acceptable.

That Ya'ari repeated this canard various times, on radio and television, and with unabashed missionary zeal, emphasized the tendentious nature of the message. Perhaps the U.S. administration was so upset by Shara's refusal to shake hands and its impact on the Israeli public that it decided to rationalize Syrian behavior by placing the blame on Israel.

Why Ya'ari should serve as an instrument for such inversion of history is anybody's guess.

The printed press was every bit as uniform. Particularly amusing was its search for something to remove the bad taste created by Shara's hand that didn't shake. At one point it gleefully announced that in the secrecy of the negotiation chamber, Shara and Barak did shake hands. It was a false report, generated by an eager member of Barak's entourage.

Far more serious was the deliberate distortion of Syrian pronouncements.

When Shara did not mention the mantra "June 4, 1967" in his abrasive and insulting speech at the White House, the Israeli press pounced on it as a signal of compromise. This was followed by repeated assertions that the Syrians were not insisting on returning to the 1967 lines.

But all these reports were nothing more than part of a disinformation campaign. The Syrians kept reiterating their demand for a return to the 1967 lines at every opportunity. Just this week (December 21) Shara told the London *Al-Hayat* that the first component of an agreement must be an Israeli withdrawal to the June 4 lines. And the editorials in the official government papers *Al-Ba'ath* and *Tishrin* repeated his demand specifically and explicitly. None of this was reported in Israel's ostrich media.

The *Economist* likes Barak

The vast majority of the world press likes Israeli leaders who make concessions. Even Menachem Begin, vilified as a terrorist and fanatic when he became prime minister, turned into a media darling after Camp David. Well, at least until he committed the unpardonable sin of saving the world from Saddam Hussein's nuclear bomb.

The phenomenon is so universal that no one seems to wonder why the media in democratic societies are so eager to see a democracy yield to dictatorial regimes, particularly since the same media would never dream of demanding such concessions of their own governments.

But the idea that Israeli concessions equal peace is so entrenched that it has become an accepted truth.

Yet even the sympathy and support for conciliatory

leaders cannot suppress the anti-Israel pro-Arab bias, often fed by abysmal ignorance and chronic misinformation, which afflicts some British journalists. An article by Middle East editor of the *Financial Times* David Gardner in last week's *Economist* (December 18) is a case in point.

Nauseatingly patronizing, Gardner approves of Barak's readiness to withdraw. But this does not stop him from calling Israel's prime minister "the thinking man's thug."

It is difficult to imagine that a similar reference to Tony Blair in an Israeli magazine would warm the cockles of Gardner's heart.

Like most of his colleagues, Gardner keeps referring to "Arab Jerusalem," presumably the part of the city that was under Jordanian occupation for 19 years after its Jewish population was killed or expelled, and which now has a Jewish majority.

He also refers to "historic Palestine," giving an unmistakable impression that a state named Palestine, whose capital was Jerusalem, actually existed some time in the past, and that it is now occupied by Israel.

But a peace settlement seems remote, Gardner avers, because Barak "wants [Jerusalem] off the negotiating table, as though Arabs and Moslems could acquiesce in Israel's continuing occupation of the third holiest site in Islam, the Haram ash-Sharif in the Old City, with the Dome of the Rock and the ancient al-Aksa mosque, a stone's throw from the Wailing Wall."

Leaving aside the condescending sobriquet "Wailing Wall," the passage betrays a double standard so deeply entrenched that Gardner, to give him the benefit of the doubt, may not even be aware of it.

Perhaps one day in the next century a writer with the backbone, honesty and open mind of a Benjamin Disraeli will rise in Britain. And, free of medieval biases and prejudices, he will write: "The Palestinians expect to get the Old City of Jerusalem, as though the Jews of the world and all those who share Judeo-Christian values could acquiesce in relinquishing Judaism's holiest site, the Temple Mount. How utterly offensive it is to expect Israel to give up half the city that has been the national and spiritual capital of the Jewish people for 3,000 years!"

And when that happens, we shall truly know the millennium has arrived.

The Battle for Jerusalem
January 7, 2000

If the activities of "peace camp" followers is any indication, the propaganda campaign for the division of Jerusalem has gone into high gear.

One of the more blatant recent efforts is a tract of political propaganda issued as an advertising supplement in *The Jerusalem Post* by B'Tselem, a branch of the "peace camp" masquerading as a human rights organization.

The very name of this organization, "The Israeli Information Center for Human Rights in the Occupied Territories," betrays its political bias. Only those who ignore the principles of international law for the sake of Israel-bashing refer to Judea, Samaria and Gaza as "occupied territories." The only time these areas were illegally occupied was in the years 1948-1967, when they were under Jordanian rule.

That B'Tselem also refers to Jerusalem, Israel's capital under Israeli law, as "occupied territory" can only mean that it is an outright mouthpiece for the PLO, not a human rights organization.

The 16-page B'Tselem tract, named "Injustice in the Holy City," meticulously avoids rebuttals by government or municipal authorities to its claims. Both Mayor Olmert and the monograph "Arab building in Jerusalem" by Israel Kimhi of the Jerusalem Institute for Israel Studies have refuted most of B'Tselem's allegations.

But it must be said that the B'Tselem supplement does have a certain nostalgic value.

With a few changes of time and place it could pass for a 1970 Soviet pamphlet describing the insufferable hardship of life in the West, complete with statistics, personal testimonies and statements by fellow travelers.

The inconvenient question the Soviets used to ignore - if life in the West is so bad, how come everyone in the East wants to move there? - is applicable in this case too.

If all the B'Tselem horror stories about the treatment of Palestinians in Jerusalem are true, how come the growth of the city's Arab population outpaces that of the Jewish population? And how come there is more Arab building per capita in Jerusalem than Jewish building? Half of the Arab buildings are illegal (mostly because it is cheaper and faster to build without permits), but only a negligible number are demolished.

If anything, Israel is guilty of Third World laxity on this issue.

The purpose of the publication is clear enough. By pointing out that parts of today's municipal area used to be Arab villages (how is this the business of a human rights organization?), B'Tselem is advocating turning them over to Palestinian rule. It is a solution known since 1996 as the Beilin-Abu Mazen plan (though neither Abu Mazen nor any other Palestinian has ever agreed to it).

According to this plan, the areas transferred to Palestinian rule would be called Al Quds, the Arabic name for Jerusalem (few realize that this name, which means "the holy," refers to the city's sacredness to the Jews). And, voila, you have two Jerusalems, two capitals existing peacefully side-by-side.

Of course, no Palestinian leader would be willing to consider anything less than the whole area once occupied by Jordan, particularly the Old City, as the Palestinian capital. But getting the Israeli public used to the idea of shedding parts of Jerusalem like Beit Hanina that, as B'Tselem puts it, "most Israelis have never heard of," is a step in what this organization considers the right direction.

Moreover, it is an effective technique for dismantling the whole state.

After all, how many Israelis have heard of the names of Arab villages in the Galilee, the Negev, and the Triangle? Using Palestinian logic, as B'Tselem invariably does, leads to the inevitable conclusion that all the land is "occupied," and that Israel has no right to exist.

Israel will most likely survive this assault on its legitimacy. But the Palestinians will always owe B'Tselem, and other components of the "peace camp," an eternal debt of gratitude for helping them achieve a carefree existence in the happy land of the PLO, where freedom, justice and respect for human rights reign.

Another effort to dismantle Jerusalem is being made in The Museum of the Seamline, in a building owned by the municipality near the Mandelbaum Gate.

Initially dedicated to the unity of Jerusalem and the heroism of its liberators, the museum is now devoted to fighting violence. And to make sure its message is understood, it allows visitors to view the exhibits only if accompanied by a guide.

Former Harvard Business School professor and author Dr. Carol Greenwald describes a visit to this anti-violence museum in a newsletter she publishes in Bethesda, Maryland, called *Israel Action Alert*. It is not the kind of description found in the Israeli press.

"One film clip of violence scans between Northern Ireland, South Africa, and the bus bombings in Jerusalem. But the scenes are so rapid that one is never clear who is doing violence to whom, except when the camera slows to show an Israeli soldier or policemen beating an Arab. But one never knows who the victims and the aggressors are.

"It is the visual equivalent of Bill Clinton's statement that the orphans of those killed by terrorist bombers and the children of the terrorists were all victims.

"There is also a 10-minute movie about the diversity of Jerusalem. But nowhere does it indicate that Jerusalem is in Israel, and that only as Israel's capital has there been religious freedom for all peoples in Jerusalem.

When asked if the point of the movie was that Jerusalem belongs to the world, the guide said, "Of course."

"On the roof of the building the guide pointed out the sites on the skyline. 'Over there,' he said, 'is Mr. Scopus and Hadassah Hospital, where the myth of the doctors dying took place.' 'Myth?!' I shouted. 'That's not a myth! Were not 77 doctors and nurses murdered by Arab gunmen?' 'Everyone has their own interpretation of facts,' he replied. 'That is what makes it a myth.' 'No,' I insisted. 'Is it not true that they were killed?' The guide finally conceded that doctors and nurses had died on that road. He could not bring himself to utter the word 'killed.'"

And then there is "Jerusalem 2000," a Yediot Aharonot fashion supplement in which winter fashions were shown against 12 different backgrounds in Jerusalem. These include the Nablus Gate, a large cross at an unidentified church, an Arab shoe-shiner, an Arab grocery, an entrance to an Arab home, the Church of all Nations (Gethsemane), various staircases in the Moslem Quarter, the Dome of the Rock, a park in an Arab neighborhood, Orient House, and (surprise!) the menora at the Knesset.

Divide Jerusalem? If this supplement is any indication, the Jews should consider themselves lucky to receive one-twelfth of it.

Those who believe that if only parts of Jerusalem become a Palestinian capital peace will come to the holy land may want to peruse the minutes of a symposium in Gaza, held on December 27 and never mentioned in the Israeli press.

The participants, ministers of the Palestinian Authority and Palestinian scholars, included PA Finance Minister Mohammed Zehdi Nashashibi, history lecturer in Gaza's Islamic University Dr. Atham Sislam, former head of the Palestinian team in the Madrid talks Haider Abdel Shafi, and Jerusalem legislator Hatem Abdel Kader. They all agreed that Jerusalem cannot be "liberated" by negotiations. Only a return to the struggle can retrieve "every inch of Jerusalem."

An additional point, which is becoming a regular feature of Arab propaganda, is that the historic Jewish presence in Jerusalem is a myth.

"The archeologists have found no proof of Jewish existence in Jerusalem," states Nashashibi, who refers to the Temple as "a fake." Chimes in history professor Sislam: "Research proves that the Jews have no history in Jerusalem."

Can anyone wish for more likely peace partners?

Out of Sight, Out of Mind
January 21, 2000

The fashionably liberal British daily *The Guardian* is the epitome of political correctness on Israel, which is another way of stating that while it clearly prefers Israel's Labor party to any alternative, its first loyalty is to the PLO. Although not quite as one-sided as it used to be, it seldom bothers to present the Israeli side. Only one major British daily, *The Independent*, is more biased. Its weekly magazine of January 1 was devoted to photographs of the century. Called "One Hundred Years in Pictures," it contains some remarkable photos. But even more remarkable is that this 92-page survey of the century never mentions Israel.

Even Jews, it seems, barely exist in the 20th century. They are mentioned only once, in a section called "War, Again." A caption of a photograph reads: "1943, German troops clear the Warsaw ghetto. After a month of bitter house-to-house combat, Jewish resistance fighters were overcome by vastly superior forces. Of the 56,000 Jews rounded up by the Nazis, 7,000 were executed and the remainder sent to death camps."

This is the extent of the Jewish role in the century. Even the caption of a picture of trenches filled with bodies in Bergen Belsen fails to mention Jews. "1945, BelsenBritish troops entered the camp in April 1945. They found 35,000 bodies and another 30,000 inmates near death. In the days following the liberation many hundreds more died from disease or starvation."

Not that *The Guardian* ignores the truly important events in the Middle East.

Under the heading "New Frontiers," it has the following pictures: the Eiffel Tower at the Paris Exposition in 1900, Orville Wright's Kitty Hawk, Pavlov's laboratory, The

Millennium Dome, the first Soviet cosmonaut, the first Vatican radio broadcast, the first image transmitted by wireless, the first space suit, the explosion of the space shuttle Challenger, the WWII Japanese invention of anti-aircraft listening devices, Amelia Earhart's cross-Atlantic solo, the Berlin airlift, Neil Armstrong's boot print on the moon, and the first hydrogen bomb test.

All eminently legitimate illustrations of breakthroughs. But *The Guardian* obviously felt something was missing. So to complete the series, it included a photo of yet another glorious event that demonstrated man's infinite inventiveness and bold imagination. "1970, the first of three passenger jets, hijacked by terrorists of the Popular Front for the Liberation of Palestine and flown to a remote airstrip in Jordan, is blown up."

There is, to be sure, a section called "Terror" where such a photograph would have been appropriate, but no Palestinians are included in this one.

On the other hand, a section on "Protest" has "1993, Palestinians protest for the right of self-determination on the walls of old Jerusalem." Even here *The Guardian* manages to avoid the word Israel. As far as *The Guardian* is concerned, Jerusalem, like no other capital in the world, is a city in limbo belonging to no country.

The Palestinian leadership has a different idea. On a recent tour for a visiting Jewish group at Orient House, Palestinian official Rami Tahboub announced: "Jerusalem has been the capital of the Palestinian people for more than 5,000 years."

To combat Israel's biblical claim to the Land of Israel, Palestinians no longer declare that they are part of the great Arab nationas they used to do before the establishment of Israel, when only Jews were called Palestinians. Now they trace their lineage to the Jebusites, Canaanites, Philistines, and all the other tribes displaced by the Israelites according to the Bible.

That they also claim that the Bible stories are fiction does not seem to bother them. Nor are they perturbed by the fact that such ancestry would mean that they are not Arabs, and that the Arab invasion of the 7th century was a foreign occupation. Logic and history are irrelevant to this myth-weaving.

More than eight years ago Hanan Ashrawi signaled this new direction of Arab propaganda when she announced in Madrid that she was a descendant of the first Christians. This would make her a Jew, a distinction she would probably be less than happy to claim.

But the 200 Western journalists who cheered her at the time did not quite see it that way. With what can only euphemistically be described as an uncontrollable urge to trash anything Israeli, these journalists, mostly brought up on the Bible, accepted the declaration uncritically. Just as they do when Arafat refers to Jesus, a Jew born in Judea according to the New Testament, as "a Palestinian," a term that did not exist at the time. Nor do they guffaw at a headline in one of the PA's papers, *The Jerusalem Times*: "Christmas Tree revered as a national symbol in Palestine."

Science, history, and enlightenment are clearly no match for the willingness of some journalists to be fooled by intelligence-insulting slogans. If a higher goal is to be served, let the truth be damned.

Not one journalist remarked on the ludicrousness of the announcement by MK Hashem Mahmeed, member of the Knesset Foreign Affairs and Defense Committee, who introduced himself at a NATO meeting in Brussels last November as "a Palestinian Arab who is a member of the

Palestine Knesset."

Such fecund flights of the imagination are mostly absent from the sophisticated office diary published by The Palestinian Academic Society for the study of International Affairs (PASSIA).

Unlike previous publications by PASSIA, the 2000 diary keeps its propaganda subtle. Handsomely designed and well organized, it actually makes a few concessions to reality.

While the title of one of its maps, "The Palestinian Metropolis within the limits of Greater Jerusalem," is puzzling, the map itself is accurate. It even uses the Hebrew name Har Homa for the controversial hill in the southern part of the city. Even more surprising is that the name Israel appears on three of the maps, which is more than can be said about maps used in Palestinian schools.

To be sure, history is told from a Palestinian viewpoint, and it is highly selective. Referring to the assassination of King Abdallah in Jerusalem, for example, it is careful to omit the Palestinian identity of his assassin. But it does state that the Palestinians rejected the UN resolution recommending the establishment of Jewish and Arab states, a rare admission for Palestinian Arabs.

Nor can it be blamed for emulating Israel's own rewriters of history, the "new historians," when describing the war as a confrontation between "well-equipped and trained Zionist army fighting against poorly armed Palestinian resistance groups."

There is a refreshing respectability about this 350-page diary, which shuns the insane Big Lies repeated ad nauseam by Arafat and his coterie. Its relative sanity may make it a more effective propaganda tool, but there is always hope where truth is allowed a foothold.

Time corrects

On December 3 this column cited the *Time* report on Suha Arafat's speech charging Israel with causing cancer in Palestinian women and children with poison gas. *Time* did not quite buy the cancer part, but asserted that tear gas was linked to miscarriages in Palestinian women.

This was a particularly piquant libel because it was published even as American police were using tear gas against demonstrators in Seattle.

The Boston-based media watch organization CAMERA protested, and *Time* published a correction in its January 17 issue, stating, "There are no scientific studies that show any link between tear gas and miscarriages."

David Bar-Illan Hospitalized After Heart Attack
February 27, 2000

Jerusalem Post columnist David Bar-Illan suffered a massive heart attack at his Jerusalem home on Friday night. He was rushed to Shaare Zedek Hospital, where he is in the intensive-care unit.

Bar-Illan, 70, was executive editor of the *Post* between 1992 and 1996, when he became director of policy planning and communications for then Prime Minister Binyamin Netanyahu. He returned to the paper as a columnist last year.

Jerusalem: The Burdensome Stone
By Thomas S. McCall, ThD, *Levitt Letter*, April 1996

Jerusalem, the Holy City, the City of the Great King, God's Holy Hill of Zion, the Center of the Earth, the Cup of Trembling, the Burdensome Stone, Sodom and Gomorrah, and Egypt. Jerusalem is called by these and many other names in the Bible. As Israel and the P.L.O., under international pressure, enter into the most critical aspect of the current "peace process," which is the effort to make a permanent settlement concerning Jerusalem, many claims and issues must be dealt with.

To Whom Does Jerusalem Belong?

The Jews say it belongs to Israel. It was the political capital and Temple worship center of the ancient Commonwealth for over 1,000 years, has been the spiritual home of the Jewish people ever since, and is understood to be the future capital of the Messiah.

The Arabs say it belongs to Islam. It is the third most sacred place to Moslem believers, next to Mecca and Medina. The city was under Moslem control from the seventh century until World War I, with the one-century exception during the Crusades.

The Papacy says it belongs to Christendom. Jerusalem is sacred to Christians because of both Old and New Testament associations, and is the site of the death and resurrection of Christ. The holy sites are of great concern, of which the Church of the Holy Sepulchre is supreme.

The United Nations says it belongs to the world. Jerusalem is revered by the world's three great monotheistic religions, and is critical as a hot spot that could well endanger world peace. Therefore, the U.N. wants to "internationalize" the city, so that no one ethnic or religious group would have control.

Jerusalem Under Israel and Jordan

What should the attitude be among those of us who believe in the Lord Jesus Christ and are evangelicals? Our conviction is that all of the Land of Israel, including Jerusalem, belongs to the Jewish people by divine decree, and we should recognize their rights of ownership. During the last three decades, in which most of the Land has been under Israeli control, evangelical Christians have had full and free access to just about all of the country. Christian tourists have been welcome, and there has been no problem seeing all of the marvelous biblical sites. The holy places of all religions are kept sacrosanct, and Jews, Moslems and Christians may visit these places and rest assured that no important site will be desecrated.

Such could not be said when the country in general, and Jerusalem in particular, was under Moslem control. My wife and I were in Jerusalem in 1965, on a tour with Dr. Charles Feinberg. This, of course, was before the Six-Day War in 1967, and Jerusalem was part of the Kingdom of Jordan, and ruled by King Hussein. East and West Jerusalem were separated by a jagged zone called "no man's land." The Mandelbaum Gate was the only way anyone could get from one side to the other. It was like Checkpoint Charlie in Berlin. As a practical matter, no civilians could pass from Israel into Jordan, and about the only civilians who could pass from Jordan to Israel were foreign tourists. Once Christians got into Jordan, they could visit most of the New Testament holy places, but getting to Jordan was a serious problem, and the problem was created by the unwillingness of Jordan to cooperate with Israel.

As the Jordanians would not allow tourists to go from Israel into Jordan, we had to go to Jordan first, via Egypt, and then go into Israel through the Mandelbaum Gate. When Jerusalem was divided, it was difficult for pilgrims to visit the many important biblical sites.

The Western Wall Under Moslem Control

The entire Old City in 1965 was in Jordan, along with most of the biblical sites. This included the Dome of the Rock, the Temple Mount and the Western Wall. One of the places we wanted to visit was the Western Wall, sometimes called the Wailing Wall. Those who are familiar with the Wall as it is today, with its spacious plaza and daily crowds of people who come to worship and pray, can scarcely imagine what it was like in 1965. In actuality, it was a slum. The Arab houses were built up to within about ten feet of the Wall, and the space between was like an alley. Really, it was worse than that, because all around were the odors of a latrine. The Western Wall, closed in as a dank alleyway, was deserted then. No Jews were praying at this most sacred of sites to Judaism. No young boys were performing their Bar Mitzvah rites of reading the Torah, with all their admiring family rejoicing at the Wall. It was deserted when Jordan had control of the Old City. No Jews were allowed at the Western Wall for about 20 years.

Transformation of Jerusalem Under Jewish Control

What a difference when Israel recaptured the Old City in 1967. Within months, the old slum was cleared away from the

Wall, a grand plaza was established, and hundreds to thousands of people began gathering there daily to pray and worship the God of Abraham and Moses.

Once Jerusalem was reunited under Jewish control, the Moslems had free and total access to the Dome of the Rock, the Al Aksa Mosque, and all their holy places throughout the Land. Christians also, including evangelicals, have had complete and unfettered access to all the important places in Israel, including the Temple Mount, the Church of the Holy Sepulchre, the Garden Tomb, the Mount of Olives, and all the Sea of Galilee.

One shudders to think of what might happen if Jerusalem were again to be taken out of the hands of the Jewish people, even if it were placed under the U.N. or the Papacy, much less the P.L.O. Both evangelical Christians and Jews could well find themselves having much-reduced access to the scriptural sites. Furthermore, God never gave legal title of Jerusalem to Moslems or Christians or the United Nations. He gave the legal right to Jerusalem to Abraham and his descendants through Isaac and Jacob. What right do we have to try to nullify this grant to Israel from the Lord?

The Push to Remove Jerusalem from Israeli Control

Our conviction, therefore, is that both the scriptural mandates and the interests of Jews and evangelical Christians (and peace-loving Arabs, for that matter) are best served by Jerusalem remaining in the hands of Israel until the Lord returns. Already, for years, our U.S. government under two administrations and the U.N. have applied pressure on Israel to surrender strategic territory to Moslem interests. In spite of the strong reservations of many Jews and evangelical Christians, it appears that our various governments may well try to remove Jerusalem from Israeli control. This is very regrettable, and we should resist such efforts wherever possible. Nevertheless, as the Bible teaches that Jerusalem will be a cup of trembling and a burdensome stone for all the nations in the End Times (Zech. 12:2-3), we should not be surprised.

Jerusalem: The Cup of Trembling
By Zola Levitt, *Levitt Letter*, September 2000

At the time of this writing, Yasser Arafat has completed a trip through Europe, including Russia, looking for support to declare his new state. I don't know if he will do that on September 13, but if he does, it will be another of those Palestinian propaganda initiatives.

One has only to spend some time in Israel watching the Israelis and the Palestinians living their daily lives to conclude who really owns the land, who loves the land, who works the land, and who ought to have the land.

An unsaved Jewish friend pointed out to me that 25 years ago I told him there would be some unholy alliance against Israel headed up by Russia (the invasion of Gog and Magog in Ezekiel 38 and 39). He reminded me that Arafat meeting Putin, the "president" of Russia, may lead to such excessive anti-Semitism as an actual invasion of the Holy Land.

God's will is clear on that. He gave Israel to Abraham and his seed after him through Isaac, Jacob, etc., down to the modern Jewish people. His promise of restoration of the Jews to Israel does not depend on their behavior or even their faith. It is simply an immutable, everlasting promise He made to His friend, Abraham, and of course, it is still in force. In fact, we are living in the generation that saw the fulfillment of this breathtaking prophecy of some 3,500 years range. Deuteronomy 30, among many other passages, cites God's intention of restoring His Chosen People to the Promised Land, and that was given during the Exodus! A 3,500-year-old promise is not to be taken lightly.

And who would have guessed that our modern church would be so far out of step as to fail to see this amazing fulfillment, even as it happens before our very eyes. I mean, after all, what are the odds that the Jewish people without God would ever even have survived this long, let alone be restored to their ancient land? How likely is it that God is really working through the American church, or your denomination or mine, or some body of churchmen, however sincere, when He has always worked through Israel and promised to do that until eternity?

And I guess it doesn't stop there, because eternity will create a new heaven, a new earth, and you know what city...a new Jerusalem! When our tourists arrive in the Holy City, I tell them in my first talk that they're looking at a city that will never perish, not ever, not for eternity!

Our seminaries and our churches teach it otherwise. Israel is of little importance in a majority of churches and in the large seminaries, and we have belabored that point, I know. But frankly, this will be a life-long mission of mine because I am a Christian (not because I am a Jew). A Christian is a believer in the Jewish Messiah, who is on his way to Israel for a 1,000-year stay in the Kingdom to come. A Christian is one who is passionately interested in his future homeland and the land of the patriarchs, the prophets, and the Messiah. A Christian is respectful of the Chosen People, whom God loves, and takes their part when they are embroiled in political discourses, election campaigns, and every other worldly situation, from anti-Semitism to all-out war. A

Christian is one who has a ready answer to the Lord's provocative question in the judgment of the sheep and the goats at the beginning of the Kingdom: "How did you treat my (Jewish) brothers?" (see Matt. 25:40). And a Christian is one who is most skeptical of the unbelievers' posturing at "peace conferences" and the like.

President Clinton is simply not believable, and Yasser Arafat obviously doesn't want peace. The exasperated Israelis can't seem to give away enough to appease their myriad antagonists, and the whole peace process is at a standstill, and well and good. It would never have led to peace in any case, but I hope we can stop pretending for now. Once Clinton is out of office, I think all of this rushing about and negotiating will die off. It is increasingly clear that the Arabs don't want land for peace, they just want the land, all of it.

I don't mean to sound disheartened about all this since, truly, it is what is to be expected in End Times prophecy. The chapters of Ezekiel discussing the "dry bones" vision and the Russian invasion read as one continuous story, implying that, once the Jews are back in the land, the trouble starts, and indeed it has. We are rapidly approaching the moment when Jerusalem will become the "burdensome stone" and the "cup of trembling" that Zechariah holds it to be at the end. It does seem like the whole world is burdening itself with the problem of Jerusalem (as if there really were a problem), and nobody can seem to solve the dilemma (whatever the dilemma is).

American Airlines Flying Higher
By Zola Levitt, *Levitt Letter*, August 2002

Many of you have responded to our call that American

Airlines correct the offensive reference to "Held Territories" in its mailings to customers who live in Jerusalem. Because of this exposure and your determination to get involved, American has finally reversed itself.

From the beginning, American has been apologetic about what it termed a "computer glitch." However, the explanations about misprints and internal codes, etc. just didn't satisfy us that the airline was taking this error seriously.

After correspondence and phone calls, American finally issued a statement on June 28, indicating that it would research a "globally recognized" source to determine the correct name for the nation of Israel in future mailings.

This apparent backtracking from earlier statements was disconcerting at best. *WorldNetDaily*, an international news site with a daily readership of 2.5 million, posted a front-page article about this fiasco with American.

On July 15, we contacted American once more, requesting their response to the media coverage, as well as an explanation for listing the non-nations of Gaza, Held Territories, and West Bank in their country lists on the AA website. We received the following reply from American several days later:

> The United States Postal Service advised us that addresses for cities in Israel should have Israel as the noted country. We have updated our Website and AADVANTAGE database accordingly. Again, we apologize if we've offended anyone and thank you for bringing this to our attention. We consider this topic closed.

The Postal Service is apparently a good source of information, too, since it lists Bethlehem, East Jerusalem, Gaza, Jerusalem, Ramallah, etc. as cities in Israel. It reminds me of the courtroom climax in the classic movie, "Miracle on

42nd Street." The Postal Service ultimately identified Santa Claus!

Now that some resolution has come about with American Airlines, we've recently been alerted that Marriott Hotels has joined those who cast dispersion on Israel's right to exist. In a recent letter to a prominent Israeli travel agency, Marriott addressed the letter to "Jerusalem, Occupied Palestinian Area." The representative for the hotel chain in Israel is a Palestinian; the Marriott family is Mormon. Whenever I have stayed in Marriott hotels during my travels, I have always found the book of Mormon in the nightstands. For Zion's sake, do not keep silent!

From the Editor

Jerusalem is God's beloved city. More than the capital of Israel, it is an eternal city with a history that reaches back over 3,000 years, and that will stretch forward into the Millennial Kingdom and beyond. Jerusalem, and the nation of Israel, is worth defending.

David Bar-Illan has, like few others in the media, devoted his life and career to the defense of the truth when it comes to Israel. Whether performing on concert stages as an important piano soloist, editing the *Jerusalem Post*, or as spokesman for former Israeli Prime Minister Benjamin Netanyahu, Bar-Illan has maintained his focus on his beloved Israel.

Fighting courageously with his pen as his sword, Bar-Illan motivates us all the more to support that tiny democracy which God has chosen. Although illness has stilled his pen, and he is enjoying a well-deserved retirement in Jerusalem, the effect of his writing will continue to challenge all who love the Chosen People and the Promised Land. *Pray for the peace of Jerusalem.*

About the Author

David Bar-Illan served as executive editor of *The Jerusalem Post* between 1992 and 1996, when he became director of policy planning and communications for then Prime Minister Benjamin Netanyahu

Bar-Illan is the former publisher and editor of the Tel Aviv Hebrew weekly *La'Inyan*. From 1984 to 1989 he was the director of the Jonathan Institute, a private foundation named after Jonathan Netanyahu and dedicated to combating international terrorism.

His columns and articles have appeared in numerous publications in the United States, Europe and Israel including *The Wall Street Journal, The New York Times, The New York Post, The Los Angeles Times, Newsweek, Saturday Review, Commentary, Global Affairs* and *The London Daily Telegraph.*

He has lectured on the Middle East at universities and various organizations, and has appeared on U.S. Radio and television programs, including the *MacNeil/Lehrer Report, Crossfire, Good Morning America* and CBS *Nightwatch.* In 1995-1986, he hosted a weekly public affairs program, *International Dateline*, on cable television in the U.S.

He is a recipient of the Liberty Medal of the City of New York, awarded on the occasion of the restoration of the Statue of Liberty.

Bar-Illan is a concert pianist who has appeared as soloist with most of the world's major orchestras and has recorded extensively.

He now lives in Jerusalem with his wife Adina (Beverly). They have five children.

For further study, consider these publications available at Zola Levitt Ministries:

Books

Jerusalem Forever (JF) - *New!*
Prophecy at Ground Zero (PGZ) - *New!*
Glory (GLO)
Israel: Past and Present (IPP)

Videos

Jerusalem 3000 (VJER)
This is Israel (VTI)
Upon This Rock (VUTR)

Other

"Pray for the Peace of Jerusalem" Bumper Sticker (BS)
Map of Jerusalem (MOJ)

Subscribe to our free monthly newsletter, *The Levitt Letter*, and watch Zola on his television program, *Zola Levitt Presents*, which airs nationally on ABC-FAM, TBN, and on hundreds of local stations. Call or write for a free airing schedule.

Join Zola on one of his many tours to Israel, Greece, and to Biblical sites in the United States. Contact Travel Experience International at (214) 696-9760 for brochures and itineraries.

For more information or for a free catalog of ministry materials, please contact:

Zola Levitt Ministries
P. O. Box 12268
Dallas, TX 75225
(214) 696-8844
1-800-WONDERS
www.levitt.com